Newsletter Marketing

Insider Secrets to Using Newsletters to Increase Profits, Get More New Customers, and Keep Customers Longer than You Ever Thought Possible

Shaun Buck

NEWSLETTER MARKETING: Insider Secrets to Using Newsletters to Increase Profits, Get More New Customers, and Keep Customers Longer Than You Ever Thought Possible

Copyright © 2013 Shaun Buck. All rights reserved.

www.thenewsletterpro.com

ISBN: [TBD]

Printed in the United States of America

First Edition

Design and Layout by Brodie Tyler - www.doxmarketing.com

CONTENTS

Dedication

Thank you, Lord, for your mercy and blessings, which you give me on a daily basis.

To my beautiful wife, Mariah: Thank you for the love and support you've shown me over the years. I am so glad we are taking the rest of this journey through life together. Also, thank you for being such an awesome mom to our five boys. I love you.

To Brandon: It has been a crazy, fun, and exciting 17 years since you were born. I could never have imagined back then how great a young man you would become. I owe much of my success to having you in my life, and I want you to know that I love you very much and am proud of the man you are becoming.

To Tyler: If there was ever such a thing as a born entrepreneur, it is you. You are funny, handsome, smart, and charismatic. I enjoy watching you grow every day. Keep up the great job you are doing of being a big brother to all of your little brothers. They look up to you, and for good reason.

To Jeremiah: Your smile and laugh can melt my heart. You are so sweet, and one of the best parts of my day is when I come home and you run over and give me an excited hug and a kiss. I hope you always stay Daddy's boy.

To Alexander: You are such a sweet and handsome little boy. I enjoy snuggling you before bed as well as all of your other bedtime rituals. I want you to know Daddy loves you.

To Kellen, aka Duck: Your almost bald baby head and big smile for me every night while Momma gives you your last bottle of the day is one of the highlights of my day. I love you.

To my dad: Thank you for your support and friendship over the years. It may seem silly to some, but I hope I've made you proud. Also, for the record, I believe I have gone above and beyond the call of duty when it comes to keeping the family name alive and strong.

To my mom: Last of my thank-yous, but certainly not the least. Mom, I want you to know I love you, and just in case I haven't told you, I appreciate all you did for us kids growing up. You worked hard, and from my point of view, always did what you thought was in our best interest. I am not sure what more a kid could ask for. By the way, I know how much you enjoy reading, so I hope you enjoy the book—and I love you.

Special Bonus!

If you haven't already done so, start right now by going to my website to receive a FREE 12-month premium print subscription to my monthly newsletter, plus a bonus copy of one of my Gold CDs titled "5 Ways to Use Newsletters to Increase Sales and Crush Your Competition." Both complement this book well. Just go to www.TheNewsletterpro.com/book and fill in the form on the screen. We'll mail (yes, a real physical hard copy of both the newsletter and CD will be mailed to you). Go to www.TheNewsletterpro.com/book. You'll be happy you did!

CHAPTER 1
The Newsletter Pro

I have taken a different path than most to becoming an entrepreneur. I could go all the way back to being 10 or 11 years old and give the history of what drove me to want to be a business owner, but that isn't the purpose of this book and is possibly better left to someone with bigger titles and more college degrees than I have to fully analyze.

But before I jump into how you too can grow your business with newsletters, I do want to take a moment to introduce myself and give you a bit of my story because I think it is important for you to understand a little about me, my entrepreneurial philosophy, and how I ended up publishing hundreds of newsletters.

It all started when I was just a wee baby. No, I'm just kidding. Let me fast-forward a bit. In 1995, at age

16, I got a phone call that changed my life forever. My ex-girlfriend was calling to tell me she was pregnant. At first I was confused. We had been broken up for about two months, and I wondered to myself why she was calling to share this with me. My confusion ended quickly when she uttered those four magic words—the baby is yours. I thought she was joking and even told her I didn't think that was funny, but I quickly realized (when she stared crying) that it wasn't a joke at all. Of course, I had the standard questions any 16-year-old would have, like are you sure and how did this happen. Some of the questions, of course, were rhetorical, as I knew how babies were made, but at 16, you don't really think about the future and what could happen. To be fair to 16-year-olds, some people I know now at 35 don't think about what may happen in the future, so I guess it isn't just a teenage thing.

A few months after that call, I was faced with the dilemma of how I was going to help take care of a baby, go to school, and maybe even try to work things out with my baby's mama. I have always been a pretty smart guy, so it didn't take me long to realize that my job at Chuck E. Cheese, playing the mouse on the weekends and bussing tables on weekdays, and making a whopping $4.50 per hour, was not going to be much help.

So I did what anyone would do. I quickly dropped out of high school and got a "real job" selling some fancy new home computers with this new thing called a Pentium processor to power them. Doesn't it just make you feel old thinking back to 1995? Sure does me as I type this.

Good news—at the new job, I not only got health insurance after 90 days, but in my first month, I made $4,800 and won a trip to Vegas and some prize money, thanks to selling a ton of Apple computers—and even before Apple was cool, I might add. Unfortunately, I had to be 21 to claim the trip and prize money. Easy come, easy go I guess, but I still made 4,800 bucks. Not bad for a 16-year-old kid, even if I do say so myself.

I am going to fast-forward a bit, but more like the fast-forwarding on your TiVo® or DVR, where you can see a bit of what is going on but not all the details. So here goes.

I ultimately did go back to school via distance learning and charter schools and got my diploma. Woo-hoo! My baby was born—a healthy, beautiful baby boy, whom we named Brandon. As I write this, Brandon is almost 17 years old and one of the most AWESOME people I have ever had the pleasure of knowing. Things didn't work out with me and my baby's mama, but in 1999, I met the love of my life. We married and since have had four more boys. Let me hit pause here because I know what you are thinking— five boys—yes, five boys. On a side note, I have been trying to convince Mariah, my wife, that it is obvious

I only make boys so that with just a little planning we could toss this whole entrepreneur thing out and get our own TV show called Shaun and Mariah, Plus Eight Boys. Doesn't that have a good ring to it? Alright let me un-pause and get back to our story. As far as education goes, I went to Solano Community College for a bit, where I took business classes along with general education. I did not graduate from college with a degree. During my college experience was when I started what I call my first "real" business. The reason I call it real is because it was more than just cutting lawns for a few people in the neighborhood or selling pagers to the kids at school. The reason I left college is actually kind of humorous. While talking to the primary business professor at the school one day after class, he told me that he had never OWNED a business before. What? And here I was taking a class from him on business when I HAD MORE REAL-LIFE BUSINESS EXPERIENCE than he did! As you can imagine, that was the end of that. I finished the semester and never went back.

Let me slow down a little on the first real business part, as this is a business book. At the ripe old age of 21, I bought a Woody's Hot Dogs franchise for 45,000 bucks, which gave me the hot dog stand itself and the right to open a hot dog stand in front of a brand new Lowes Home Improvement store. Woo-hoo! I know 45,000 bucks is a ton of cash for a 21-year-old, but I had some money saved up and had great credit, so there you go. I won't spend a ton of time on this topic, but for some reason, people like this story so here it is. We opened August 2001 and sold over $20,000 in hot dogs and sodas that month alone. Over the coming months, we did so well that we bought another Woody's Hot Dog stand in front of another new Lowes Home Improvement store, about 30 minutes from our first location. Between the two stands, we sold $400,000 to $450,000 a year in hot dogs. That's a lot of hot dogs. So the name is Woody's Hot Dogs, and the slogan is "It's the big one baby, it's a Woody." I actually laughed reading that. Man, I am such a nerd sometimes.

Alright, back to the story. Even with great sales, I quickly realized that there were some major flaws in the business model. For example, even though I was in California, it was cold in the winter standing outside for eight-plus hours a day. The margins were slim because people were stealing from us, and on and on and on.

With all the problems and the discovery that I didn't like the hot dog stand business, I started looking for a new business and people to sell these hot dog stands to. The looking for a new franchise led me to discover newsletters.

CHAPTER 2
My First Introduction to Newsletters

When I decided to start or buy another business, I did what any young entrepreneur would do—I started requesting things like uniform franchise offering circulars and franchise agreements from a few dozen franchisors. For many, that stuff would have put them to sleep, but I enjoyed reading about these businesses, how they made money, and even all the legal mumbo jumbo. Even as a kid, I loved business and numbers. That enjoyment only grew as I got older. I know I'm weird. Along with the franchise agreements, I got all kinds of sales material and sales phone calls, but after a month or two, the sales calls had all but stopped. I don't know about other people who buy franchises, but I wasn't going to be rushed into a decision. Out of the few dozen franchises I had looked into, only one franchisor—a dry cleaning business—kept in contact with me on a regular basis, mainly via an eight- to 16-page monthly newsletter, and I loved that newsletter. It had many of the aspects that make up a GREAT newsletter. Here are a few examples:

1. Personal article from the founder of the company
2. Top 10 list of franchises
3. New franchise interview
4. Success stories from existing franchises
5. Business-building ideas and tips
6. Promotion for the upcoming franchise convention
7. Updates on new products and services the franchisor would be rolling out

It really was a very well done newsletter. On a side note, it was so well done that to this day I still have every copy.

Every time one of these newsletters came in the mail, I opened it and devoured the contents. I read it cover to cover and then gave it to my girlfriend (now my lovely wife) to read so we could talk about it. I thoroughly enjoyed getting that newsletter each month and hearing about the success others were having and seeing the top 10 lists. I even felt as though I had a personal relationship with the CEO, who happened to be one of the people who was trying to get me to part with my $20,000 and sign a 10-year contract to do business with her company. My girlfriend and I would spend hours talking about what we read, about what it would be like to own that kind of a business, and about the franchise itself.

This company's newsletter was doing nearly everything right. In fact the company was doing such a good job that I did end up buying their franchise, sooner than I had wanted to. Want to take a guess as to why I bought earlier than I had planned? I wanted to become part of the company so I could attend the annual convention. I was very excited about everything they were going to teach at the convention and felt that I would be missing out if I didn't buy early and attend. Considering the relationship I felt I had with the CEO, the excitement I felt, and the growth I read about in the articles in the newsletter about new and existing franchise owners, I couldn't help myself. That newsletter was the hook.

When I was looking to buy a franchise, I considered companies that were large and small. I was interested in a few of them but not a single franchisor other than the dry cleaning franchise I ended up buying stayed in contact with me. None of them followed up for longer than two months after I first contacted them, and ultimately, all of them missed out not only on the initial franchise fee but also on the ongoing franchise fees I paid.

Because people are ready to buy when they are ready to buy, you MUST communicate with them on a regular and consistent basis. Studies have shown that only 3% to 6% of people are in the market to make a purchase right now. By not staying top of

Business Nugget 1
People are ready to buy when they are ready to buy, not when you are ready for them to buy.

mind with your prospects, you are leaving anywhere from 94% to 97% of the potential business on the table. I don't know about you, but the idea of leaving that much business on the table sucks. However, staying in contact with prospects is the best thing that you can do. Because when they are ready to buy, guess whose newsletter just arrived in the mail?

CHAPTER 3
My First Newsletter

As you can imagine, since newsletters did so well in helping the dry cleaning franchisor sell franchises, they had a section of their contract that required you to write and publish your own two- to four-page newsletter. That was very smart of the franchisor, but what was dumb, I mean really dumb, is that they left the writing and publishing up to us franchisees.

At the time, I wasn't a writer. Heck, I was glad to have made it through English in college. I didn't know the first thing about putting together a newsletter, and the franchisor had exactly zero training for us franchisees.

My first edition was a train wreck! To be fair, almost all of my editions were train wrecks. To make sure you fully appreciate just how bad they were, let me share with you an example of one of my first newsletters:

ExtraClean.
"The Newsletter for Our Valued Customers"

Shaun Buck * P.O. Box 6687 Vacaville Ca, 95696 * 707-422-6100 * September 2002

WELCOME!

We would like to welcome all of our customers to the DRY CLEANING TO-YOUR-DOOR® (DCTYD) family. You are joining tens of thousands of other customers around the country. We appreciate your business!

Deodorant Residue

Prolonged contact with deodorants may cause permanent damage. Combined with perspiration overuse of these products or infrequent cleaning causes buildup of residue or fabric damage. Antiperspirants contain aluminum chloride, which may change the color of some dyes. Residue buildup and chemical damage can occur resulting in a permanent color change of the fabric. To prevent damage, do not overuse the product and allow it to dry before dressing. Wear dress shields with silk garments. Information From: Clothes Care Gazette No. 175

The Secret to Removing Grass Stains

Most grass stains can be removed by simple washing the item according to the care instructions, especially if the stain is fresh. But if the stain has been allowed to set or proves to be difficult to remove you may need to try other treatments.

Treat the stain as soon as possible, using a pretreatment product from your local store. Test the product for colorfastness by applying it to an unexposed area. Let the garment stand for five minutes, then rinse. If the color is affected don't use the product. Also check the label on your laundry detergent for pretreatment instructions. To remove any last traces try an all fabric bleach. Again, remember to test for colorfastness. Bleach the entire garment follow the manufacturer's instructions, then launder as usual. Of course if you still need help getting the stain out let your professional dry cleaner have a crack at it – THAT'S US! Just make a note pointing out the stain and what you've already used on the garment. We have tons of experience with these types of stains!

Where Did That Stain Come From?
"But it wasn't there before!"

Have you ever looked at a garment after cleaning and noticed spots or stains that simply weren't there when you brought it in?

We call these "invisible stains" and beverages most often cause them.

Here's what happens. Let's say you spill soda or some other beverage on your shirt and it dries clear. However upon exposure to heat, most stain will turn yellow or brown. This change in color is cause by oxidation of sugar found in most beverages. Unfortunately, this problem isn't just limited to sodas: any beverage with sugar or alcohol can cause this staining problem.

If you are not familiar with the oxidation process, Here's a simple way to understand it. Think about what happens to an apple when you peel it and leave it out for a brief time. It turns brown: this is an example of oxidation!

Another type of "invisible stain" occurs when an oily substance is exposed to heat or ages in a garment for an extended time. This type of stain can be recognized by an irregular "cross pattern" that the oil makes. Once oily substances are left to oxidize, they can become yellow or brown and are extremely difficult to remove.

Here's what you can do to help us out. Point out any stains to us, so we can treat them before subjecting the garment to heat from drying or pressing. Mark the areas with a piece of tape so we know where the stain is. Otherwise, the stain may go undetected through the cleaning process and could become permanently set in the fabric.

We have the knowledge and expertise required to handle "invisible stains." If we can get to them before they are exposed to heat, we can return your garment to you in excellent condition! So don't be afraid to tell us where and when those stains occurred!

WE APPRECIATE YOUR BUSINESS!

"America's Finest FREE Home Pick-Up NEXT DAY Delivery Dry Cleaning Service"©

Honestly, the fact that I ever published that newsletter is embarrassing. Do people in their right minds really want to read about deodorant residue or an article about invisible stains? If I could nominate this newsletter for the award of most boring newsletter, I would, and I think I would have a good chance of winning.

Eventually we figured out that being boring doesn't work and that people are not

Business Nugget 2
Even a great idea poorly executed or NOT executed at all won't get you the results you're looking for.

going to read boring articles. And if they are not going to read boring articles, they surely are not going to read a whole newsletter that is nothing but boring. I see others make this mistake all the time. One of the biggest sinners when it comes to boring newsletters are dentists. Does anyone really read a newsletter filled with stories about drilling teeth, gum disease, and tooth decay? Of course not. It is estimated that 76% of the population has some kind of fear of dentists, so in this particular case, I guarantee no one is reading those newsletters.

If you are sitting there thinking, but my business is different, let me assure you it is not. Boring is boring. No one in their right mind would be reading that dry cleaning newsletter or the newsletter from the dentist unless he was reading it as a sleep aid to cure insomnia. If you publish boring, no matter what business or industry you are in, no one is going to read it.

Business Nugget 3

The biggest sin in marketing (all kinds of marketing) is being boring. If your marketing and newsletter are boring, I have two words for you—stop it!

CHAPTER 4
8 Ways Newsletters Will Grow Your Business and Bottom Line

Who doesn't want to make more money? If you answered no, you don't want to make more money, you can skip this chapter. If you're like me and you want to grow your business, this is the chapter where I'm going to dive into the details on how a newsletter will grow your business.

Number 1 – Increase the length of time your average customer does business with you, in turn, increasing your profits on every new and existing customer.

Every month you don't communicate with your customers, the relationship value you have built will decrease. It is estimated that on average, you lose 10% or more of your overall goodwill and relationship value with each customer each month he doesn't hear from you. Within six months of not hearing from you, you are nearly on the same playing field as any one of your competitors, and your customers can be stolen away easily by any one of them with even a mildly intriguing coupon, discount, or offer. I don't know about you, but that sounds like bad news to me. The single hardest thing for ANY business to do is acquire new customers, and after they have been acquired, they can be turned to the dark side. Of course, by dark side, I mean any of your competitors. That pretty much sucks. Worse, if the last time you did business with your customers, they had a problem or what they would consider a below-average experience, the speed with which they become disenfranchised with your business is accelerated, and the ease with which

Business Nugget 4

When customers take the time to tell you about problems they are having, it is a big deal—no matter what they tell you. Treat all problems, even the problems you feel are small, as big deals when speaking with customers who brought the issue to your attention. In these situations, a personalized thank-you card and a $5 or $10 Starbucks gift card will go a long way.

a competitor's offer entices them over to the dark side is drastically increased. Guess what—it actually gets worse than that. The issue that caused the customers to feel upset may not even be an issue they shared with you. Even if they *did* bring the problem to your attention, it is entirely possible they shared it with you but told you it wasn't a big deal. So you brushed it off, only for them to receive a competitor's offer in the mail a few weeks later and they never use you again.

Those scenarios happen ALL the time in business. The problem is that many business owners either, one, don't understand retention, or, two, chalk up their retention issues to being "normal" for their industry. Some level of loss of clients is normal because people do move and die, and frankly you can't please everyone 100% of the time. But most businesses don't have any clue they have a retention problem, let alone how to fix it.

If lack of communication is a major factor in loss of customer retention, then communication is a major part of increasing retention.

By publishing a monthly newsletter, you will be able to touch your customers once a month, drastically increasing the amount of communication the average business has with its customers. And when you create a newsletter your customers enjoy reading (which I will explain how to do later in the book), you will see the length of time your customers stay with your company increase.

Many people will read the previous sentence about increasing the average length of time customers stay with their business and simply move on without giving it much more thought. But that would be a mistake. The lifetime value (LTV) of customers is a very important number for your business. Let me take a look at some basic business math and explore this concept further.

Some of the Most Important Math You Can Do to Understand and Grow Your Business

If the average customer in your business right now has a gross profit for your company of $100 per month and that same average customer typically does business with you for eight months, that makes your average customer LTV $800 in gross profit. How much would you happily spend to get more of those new customers? The correct answer is, I don't know—I need more information. But for this hypothetical situation, let's assume that if you spend $175 to get new customers and keep them for eight months, you would make a profit.

Alright now, let me take this a step further. Assume that you put in a customer retention campaign that increases the length of time your average customer stays with you by five months. Also assume that your average customer keeps making you $100 per month in gross profit, bringing your total gross profit per average customer to $1,300. Now, how much would you be willing to spend to get that customer?

In our imaginary scenario, spending $275 to get an average customer now is totally reasonable. That is a 63% increase in the amount of money you can spend to acquire a customer. With 63% more money in this case, do you think you can find additional ways to get new customers? Of course you can.

Just for fun, let me ask you this: Do you think your ability to spend money on advertising that your competitors can't afford is going to piss them off? Of course it is. Confused and upset competition is always a good thing. Remember what I said before about most people missing the massive opportunity that they could have to increase the LTV of their average customer by keeping in touch with them on a regular basis (as well as to make a lot of extra money and possibly upset some of their competition). But I don't want you to miss it; it is so important to your overall business success.

This scenario doesn't even take into account that the longer customers are with you, typically the better customers they become (which we will explore in more detail later) or the fact that average customers who are with you 63% longer present additional opportunities to refer new business to you. Of course, those numbers represent a hypothetical scenario, but in real life you will see your average customers become better customers and the number of referrals you receive from each of them will increase the longer they stay with you.

Business Nugget 5
Research has shown that for every 1% increase in customer retention, profits increase by 7%. That's like getting a raise, because your profit goes straight to the bottom line.

Number 2 – Stay top of mind.

We live in a world that is SO busy. Most of us can't even remember what we did at 2:15 p.m. three days ago, let alone remember the name of the new dentist we went to or the law firm who won us a bunch of money three months ago. But that is not what most business owners think. Most business owners think that once they have done business with them, they know who they are and everything they sell (more on the everything I sell thought process later). I hate to be the bearer of bad news, but nothing could be further from the truth.

Have you ever met someone at a party or social gathering, or even at church, and had a very nice conversation with him for 10 or 20 minutes, only to have no clue what his name is two hours later when you are telling the story? I have actually had conversations with people from church every week for months and still struggled with their names. You may think that makes me a not nice person, but I'm not doing it to be mean. The truth of the matter is, it happens to most of us, but because we are a polite society (most of the time at least), we don't talk about such things.

A study was done a few years ago by Yankelovich, a market research firm, and they estimated that a person living in a city

Business Nugget 6

"My single biggest recommendation is the use of a monthly customer newsletter. Nothing, and I mean nothing, maintains your fence better."
—Dan Kennedy

30 years ago saw up to 2,000 ad messages a day, compared to up to 5,000 today.

With as many as two and a half times more advertising messages being delivered to us as the number our parents received, it is no wonder that we can't remember the name of the law firm that settled our case 27 days ago. To make matters worse, some businesses just have hard-to-remember and even harder-to-spell names.

The fact that we can't remember is part one of a

HUGE problem we business owners face. The second part of the problem is if you're new and existing customers can't remember the name of your business, how in the world are they ever going to refer new business to you? The answer is they won't. Even worse than not getting a referral, if they can't remember your name, how are they going to do ANY business with you again? If you are thinking people aren't forgetting who you are, where you are, what you do, think again. These two reasons are enough to send a monthly print newsletter.

One type of business that is struggling greatly with this is the professional practices—doctors, dentists, and lawyers. In years past, it was nearly enough to simply hang your shingle out the front door and watch business pour in, but now that is not the case. Of course, there are many reasons for this, such as increased competition, for example. But a huge factor is lack of referrals from existing patients or clients. Of course, lack of referrals and increased competition are not just happening in the professional practices arena; they are happening to every business, everywhere. Another HUGE problem facing all business owners is increased competition. You can easily see that a 150% increase in the number of advertising messages being delivered, in and of itself, shows a massive increase in competition, which makes it more important than ever to stay top of mind with your customers. If they can't remember your name, it is nearly impossible for them to do business with you again or give you a referral.

By sending a monthly customer newsletter, you drastically increase the ability for your customers and even prospects to remember your name when it is time for them to do business with you again or give you a referral.

Business Nugget 7

A newsletter is unlike most other forms of advertising you'll use in your business. When you create a newsletter the right way, the newsletter is not perceived by your prospects and clients to be advertising. Since it is not perceived as advertising, the prospects'/clients' advertising shield is down and not filtering what they are reading as much. In turn they are paying more attention to what you are saying. They are more likely to take your advice and to see you as an expert.

Number 3 – It is far easier to sell more to existing customers than it is to find new customers.

As I talked about in point number two, by sending a monthly newsletter, you get the benefit of people being able to remember your name and, in turn, doing business with you again. In this section, I want to go over how to get those returning customers to spend more money with you.

Once you have conquered one of the single hardest aspects of business, which is to get people to open their wallets and spend real money with you, you have the start of a relationship with your new customers. Now if you prove to them that you have a good product or service and that you provide good customer service, you'll also be given a degree of trust. You'll also have a degree of familiarity, which makes the second sale to the same customers infinitely easier than the first sale. That familiarity and level of trust also increase your new, satisfied customers' willingness to spend more with you, even on higher priced products and services.

Here is the rub, though—most business owners either overlook or abuse the relationship and/or the trust that has been placed in them. It is this indifference to or abuse of the relationship that causes most business owners to lose the goodwill they have established, in turn, making selling to these customers again or selling additional products and services almost as difficult as the first sale. The indifference/abuse also has a side effect whereby these customers you have worked so hard to get become very easily poached by your competitors.

It is very important that as business owners, you

don't have an indifference to the relationship you have with your customers/prospects. Obviously, what you really want is to grow that relationship so that you have the opportunity to both service them again and sell them additional products and services.

That still begs the question, how do you use a newsletter to sell them more products or services? There are several ways to do this, but let's focus on three primary strategies.

1. Use freestanding inserts.

Being the "newsletter pro," I get to see a ton of newsletters, and one of the most common mistakes I see people make is to put blatant ads directly inside their newsletters. So there is no misunderstanding, it is not that I have a problem with the ads, but you don't want people to be reading your newsletter with their advertising shields up. Once you start putting ads in the newsletter, some people's perceptions of the newsletter change from being a publication to being an advertising piece, and that is the LAST thing you want.

So the best way to put ads in your newsletter is with what is called a freestanding insert, or FSI for short. The FSI is a separate piece of paper either stuffed into the envelope or placed into the middle of a self-mailing newsletter. We have found this insert doesn't break the sanctity of the newsletter publication itself and is the best way to put a blatant ad in your newsletter.

Of course, there are exceptions to every rule, and I want to share a story with you of one exception for one of our clients that has worked out well.

We have a client who owns a large number of retail pet store chains. On the surface, many people would say that a newsletter wouldn't work for a retail pet store, and those people would be wrong. What we did was create an eight-page newsletter for this client that has three pages of ads, the same types of ads you would normally see in the Sunday paper from a pet store or clothing company. We printed these ads directly into the newsletter and mailed them to their top few thousand customers from each store each month. They are able to track their customers' sales via rewards cards, and they found that not only are those top customers spending more in the stores per month, but they are also buying more of the advertised products. In this example, using an FSI is simply not feasible, and we have had great success with printing the ads in the newsletter in this instance. Sometimes rules are meant to be broken, but the average business is going to want to utilize FSIs instead of an ad printed directly into the newsletter.

2. Introduce new products or services.

One of my favorite ways to increase sales is by

presenting new products and/or services in the newsletter. Of course, you have to be careful that this doesn't come off as too much of a sales pitch or look like an ad. My preferred method of presenting these new products or services is via a story. You can use pretty much any story, but my favorite story to use for this type of article is one that talks about how you found, developed, or stumbled on this new product or service. The story works really well if you can also add some personal element into it.

Some people struggle with the personal side of storytelling, especially in the business-to-business world. Our newsletter is only mailed out B2B, and in Chapter 7, I have included some personal story examples that have run in our newsletter.

3. Include customer success stories.

The customer success story may be the single best way to covertly sell in your newsletter. A customer success story is exactly what it sounds like—it is a story about one or more of your current customers who have tried a product or service you offer, and it tells their results. The reason these are so successful is that not only are they stories about your product or service, but they are one big testimonial, as well. When doing a success story, there is also a very easy tie in for a pitch at the end. It may go something like this. If you want to get the same results as Suzie, all you have to do is register for our free webinar to learn more about ABC product. You could also make a blatant pitch by saying, to get your hands on the same magical stuff Suzie used to change her life go to www.TheNewsletterPro.com/book .

Can you see how, if used properly, a customer success story can be super powerful in your newsletter?

Any one or all three of the above strategies can easily help you increase sales, but they can also increase awareness or simply be used to remind people of all of the products or services your company offers. I have found that many times business owners are so close to the daily operations of their businesses that they think, well, of course, everyone knows what I do and what I sell. Unfortunately, that is not the case. I go back to the fact that people are busy, and even when it seems as though this information should be obvious, it's not.

This is a fact I was reminded of last week while I was attending a new mastermind group that I joined. I gave my introduction at the start of the day and told everyone that we create fully custom newsletters for clients, as well as a few other details of the business. About halfway through the day, I was doing a more detailed presentation on my business, when the person facilitating the group stopped me and said, "Shaun, let me make sure I understand you correctly.

You create fully custom newsletters for companies, including interviewing the business owner and ghost writing the articles, layout, and editing?" I replied, "Yes." The facilitator then asked whether anyone else understood that about my business, and six or seven people said they didn't realize that. The fact that six or seven people didn't realize that, in and of itself, wasn't surprising to me because I had only just met these people and given a 30-second introduction about my business. But when the facilitator, a guy whom I have gotten to know over the past year or so, said he didn't realize that we created fully customized newsletters for companies, that did surprise me. When I got back into the office, I checked my database and found out he wasn't on my monthly newsletter mailing list, which would explain how a guy I have known for a year or so was so taken aback by how we create newsletters for our clients.

Number 4 – Build your expert/celebrity status.

A huge benefit of publishing a newsletter is that it builds your status as an expert and a celebrity. In our culture, we have been conditioned to think of people who get published as experts or celebrities. By publishing a monthly newsletter, you increase your expert status (and, as I will explain below, you can increase your celebrity status) in the eyes of both your customers and prospects.

Let me break out being an expert and being a celebrity into two different parts of this section of the book and, in the next couple of paragraphs, focus solely on being an expert.

As a culture, we like to do business with an expert. We are even happy to pay more to an expert than we are to pay the average Joe. We also are much more likely to take the advice of an expert. Years ago, simply being doctors, dentists, or lawyers would be all that was needed to be seen as experts, but I can tell you for a fact, that is no longer true. I work with a number of these professionals, and no longer is it just because dentists tell people to have three fillings that they actually get three fillings. Many people are simply waiting until the tooth really hurts, and because of the loss of expert status, dentists have tons of patients who don't take the recommended treatments for one reason or another. The total cost to a practice can easily be hundreds of thousands of dollars in lost production. If doctors, dentists, or lawyers—people who have gone to a massive amount of school to be given those titles and be seen in the eyes of the state as an expert—are having a hard time being seen as experts, the road is much harder for us average folks.

One way to get that expert status is to be published and have your customers/prospects see the publication. The simplest way to get published is via your monthly newsletter. In the newsletter, you will have the opportunity to show you are an expert in your field above and beyond any degree you may have. To ensure all of your customers and prospects see it, all you have to do is pop a stamp on it. Plain and simple. Of course, you can't expect to be considered an expert from a single publication, but with ongoing publications, you will see an increase in people talking to you and treating you as an expert in your field.

We are a celebrity-obsessed culture. We reward celebrities with fame and riches. Some of society even takes it so far as to vote politically based on the opinions of a celebrity. As crazy as that truly is, it is the world we live in.

I want to ask you a hypothetical question. What would it do for your business if Oprah Winfrey, Donald Trump, or Lebron James endorsed your business? Obviously, your sales would skyrocket. That's why Nike and Wheaties and Coca-Cola all use celebrity endorsements. Although you may not have the marketing budget of a Nike, Wheaties, or Coca-Cola, which may keep you from hiring one of these famous people, you can always borrow celebrity and even turn yourself into a local celebrity. Whole books have been written on this topic. Since this is a book about newsletters, I am not going to get into all the ins and outs of how to do this, but I will give you an overview.

Borrowing celebrity is as simple as getting a picture taken with a famous person and telling the story of how you met. For example, this morning, I got an autograph from and my picture taken with DJ Harper, #7 of the Boise State Broncos. I fully plan to include that picture in an upcoming edition of my newsletter. In it, I will tell the story of how my kids and I met him. Now that story may not resonate with a ton of prospects or clients of mine outside of the Boise area, but it will slightly increase my celebrity with most people because I must be of some influence and importance to be meeting or hanging out with semifamous and famous people. A better story, and one I have used in the past, is when I met John Rich, from the country music group Big and Rich and winner of Celebrity Apprentice. In that story, I talk about how John and I chatted about going out to a party in Dallas that evening. A story like that is going to be much more impressive to most people and lend me more celebrity than the DJ Harper story, but it all helps.

For most businesses, simply becoming a local celebrity is good enough. To do this you need to get published in local newspapers and magazines or be interviewed on radio or TV. In most cases your appearance in these media will do little for your business, but by featuring the article or interview in your monthly newsletter you increase your local celebrity.

Number 5 – Build relationships using newsletters.

As I mentioned in Chapter 1, I used to own a

dry cleaning pickup and delivery business. When I would find people who were using another cleaner in town, I would simply go and knock on their doors and tell them about our service. Not the most fun or glamorous way to win new customers, but it worked. There was one dry cleaning owner with whom I had nearly a 100% success rate at what he said was "stealing" his customers. The reason my success rate at winning over his customers was so high was because his prices were 50% to 100% greater than my prices or anyone else's in the market and his quality and customer service didn't match his prices. But there was one exception to my near 100% ability to steal his customers. By some means, this guy had been able to build relationships, even friendships, with a larger than average group of his customers. I, of course, didn't know all of his tactics, but I did know he had some people over for dinner and went to sporting events with others. Because of those relationships, my success rate at stealing those particular customers dropped to about 10%. And, likely, the only reason I was able to able to win over that 10% of his customers was because of his crazy pricing. Of course, I showed the other 90% how I could nearly cut their dry cleaning bill in half, and I still could not get them to switch over to my service. That, my friend, is the power of a business relationship. There are a number of ways to build business relationships, one being to have one-on-one or one-on-many interactions with customers on a regular basis. One could argue that this is the best way to build not only business relationships but any relationship. I don't know about you, but if I came to my wife and told her she had to help the business by having a customer's family over for dinner every Sunday night, she might possibly make new permanent sleeping arrangements for me on the couch. The next best way to build a business relationship is with your monthly newsletter.

Still not sold on the power of the business relationship? Let me relate a story that I heard from a mentor of mine, Dan Kennedy, that illustrates the power of a business relationship.

Imagine this—you are out doing yard work on a sunny afternoon when you cut your big toe open and start gushing blood all over the place. It's obvious you're going to need stitches. Since the cut is relatively minor, you decide not to make the 30-minute trek to your doctor's office and instead stop by the doc in a box office down the street. After the doctor you just met stitches up your big toe, he listens to your heart and checks a few other things. When he is done, he looks at you and says you have to get to the hospital immediately for open heart surgery or you may die. What do you do? If you are like most people, you quickly seek a second opinion. After all, you were simply there for stitches on your big toe.

Now, let's look at this same scenario but change

the doctor from the doc in the box to the doctor whom you've been seeing for the past 20 years and with whom you have a relationship.

Now you are on the table of the doctor you have been seeing for 20 years, and after she stitches up your toe, she listens to your heart and tells you that you need to get to the hospital right away for open heart surgery or you may die. You likely would ask her if she's sure. After all, you did just come in for stitches on your big toe. But then your doctor says yes, she's sure you need to go to the hospital right now. What are you going to do? Since you know this doctor and trust her, you're going to get your rear end to the hospital right now.

That's the difference a relationship makes. But that leaves us with the question of how to build relationships with our customers. The easiest way is with a newsletter, and the easiest way to build those relationships with the newsletter is by adding a few personal stories each time. This will give people a peek behind the curtain into your life, as well as allow you to connect with them.

You might be thinking no one cares what is going on in my life or my life is too boring and mundane to write an article a month about it. I'm here to tell you that is not the case. Many people think the grass is greener on the other side, and they enjoy reading about other people's green grass. If you need proof, just look at the magazine People or the book Chicken Soup for the Soul. Both of these publications spend a lot of time focusing on regular people and their stories, and both are massively popular.

At the end of the day, people prefer to do business with people they know, like, and trust. It is your job to get people to know, like, and trust you. Short of inviting everyone over for dinner, it is hard to build those relationships on a large scale. But building relationships with your customers and prospects is one of the single most important things you can do for your business. People you have a relationship with will spend more money with you more frequently, will do business with you for longer periods of time, will refer more new customers to you, and will take more of your recommended products and/or services.

Having a relationship with your customers is HUGE, and the single best way to have a relationship with a large group of people is via a monthly newsletter that they open and read.

Number 6 – Newsletters help build your brand.

I am not normally a huge fan of building a brand. I have found that building a brand takes a ton of time and money, both things most small business owners like us lack. But, as an added bonus, by publishing a monthly newsletter, you are getting many of the benefits of a brand in the mind of your customers.

Number 7 – Newsletters have staying power.

A good newsletter is unlike other advertising if you do it right. People don't see the newsletter as an advertisement at all but instead as a publication, and you know what people do with publications? They keep them. Because newsletters are perceived as a publication, you will find many people will have months of your newsletters just laying around. I recently had one client tell about a customer of his that loves his newsletter so much that she has made a binder up just for his newsletter and that she saves every issue. How would you like for a customer or prospect to enjoy reading your publication so much that she saves every issue? When this customer needs more of his services, whom do you think she is going to call? Do you think this person is going to price shop my client, when she has kept every issue of his newsletter to date? Of course not. He has her as a customer possibly for life. The staying power of newsletters is massive and helps increase many of the areas I have already talked about, for example, referrals, the ability to sell more products and services to existing customers, branding, and so much more.

Number 8 – Newsletters have pass-around value.

One of the things I love most about newsletters is their pass-around value. When you include valuable content in your newsletter, there's always the opportunity for people to give your newsletter to friends, family members, or associates to read. Of course, when they hand off your newsletter, they are also giving you an endorsement. A client of mine, Dr. Aldon Hilton, a dentist, recently told me about how his newsletter got passed around and the results.

A prospect of his had been getting his newsletter for months, and one day on the golf course, Dr. Hilton's prospect was hanging with a golfing buddy when they started talking about the golfing buddy's son. The son needed some dental work and wasn't sure where to go to get help for his specialized problem. Dr. Hilton's prospect remembered reading a story in the most recent newsletter, and after their golf game, went to his car to get the newsletter, and gave it to his golfing buddy. The golfing buddy then gave the newsletter to his son, who then made an appointment and ended up spending just over $8,000 with Dr. Hilton.

Had Dr. Hilton simply sent an ad to his prospect, there was no way that prospect would have kept the ad. And there was little likelihood that Dr. Hilton's prospect would have said anything to his golfing buddy and almost no chance the golfing buddy would have told his son. This is not an isolated story, either. I hear stories similar to this all the time. All you have to do to get good pass-around value from your newsletter is to provide great value. Then naturally your customers and prospects will share your publications with family and friends.

* * *

There is no doubt the power of the newsletter to grow a business, retain customers, and increase referrals. And the best part is you can get all eight of the benefits we spoke about with a single monthly newsletter. No need to use six different strategies to get only one or two of the benefits we talked about.

But now that you understand how powerful newsletters are, let's look into the mechanics of putting together a successful monthly newsletter.

CHAPTER 5
How to Create a Monthly Newsletter

When we first sign up a new client, we spend a lot of time planning the newsletter. We take a close look at who is going to be receiving the newsletter, and then we plan our content around that person.

Let me give you an example. One of our regular newsletters is from a personal injury attorney to all the chiropractors in his area. The type of people who will be receiving the newsletter varies because we never know who in the office is going to read the newsletter before the doctor sees it. Also, we can't always be 100% sure who is giving out the referral: Is it the doctor or is it the office manager?

However, what we do know is that the goal of the newsletter is for the doctors to read it, so we want to give them valuable information. In this scenario, during our planning and strategy session, we would want to make sure a portion of the newsletter is dedicated to content that will help the chiropractor grow or improve her practice. We would also want to endear the chiropractor, as well as the office staff, to the attorney, who wants to receive the referral. Additionally, we would also want to include a section with some fun in it, which likely will be for both the chiropractor and her office staff.

At this point, we would estimate how much content those sections will require and then brainstorm for additional sections that would be appealing to our target audience.

Once we have an idea of the type of sections we are going to have or an estimate of how long each article will be, we double check that the sections we have created will be of interest to our target audience, which in this case is the chiropractor and her office staff.

The scenario I used is an example of a B2B newsletter. Many times, when I see B2B newsletters, they are all stuffy and boring. It is almost as if people who are selling to other businesses actually believe they are selling to the business. Nothing could be further from the truth. Just like in B2C, at the end of the day, a person, not the business, buys the product. If you remember back to the start of the book, I told you the number one sin in all of marketing was being boring, and most B2B newsletters I see are boring. Whatever you do when creating your newsletter, DON'T BE BORING!

About a year ago, I had a client, who is also a friend of mine, who wanted to do newsletters. We were selling in a B2B market. We went through the process of planning his newsletter, and he and his wife reluctantly agreed on the nonbusiness content we suggested. As we started to produce the news-letter, he started removing more and more of the B2B content and asked us to create additional very boring content that was all industry specific informa-tion and wanted to replace the fun and interesting content we had already created. This newsletter was quickly becoming a disaster and, I knew, before we ever printed a single issue, that in the long run, there was no way this newsletter was going to get him the desired results. So, although he is a friend, I ended our business relationship. We have published a number of B2B newsletters over the years, and to this day, fun and interesting ones always outperform the boring ones for one simple fact—no one reads the boring newsletters.

CHAPTER 6
Design and Layout

I am by no means a graphic designer, and I don't even pretend to be one. But I do know both good and bad graphic design when I see it. Most newsletters fall in the bad graphic design category. Hopefully, with these tips, your newsletter will be interesting and appealing to the eye, and will encourage instead of discourage readership. Below are areas of graphic design that you have to figure out and possibly get help on to publish a successful newsletter.

1. Color or black and white (B&W)

You have heard the saying a picture is worth a thousand words, right? Well, the full thousand words don't all apply to B&W pictures. Your newsletter should be printed in color because you lose so much by printing in B&W. I have found that people typically feel that most B&W newsletters are dull. Personally, the only circumstance in which I would use a B&W newsletter is if it were a paid newsletter subscription, and even then, I would likely use color. At the end of the day, a B&W newsletter is better than no newsletter, but upgrade to color as soon as possible.

2. Masthead and footer

Your newsletter should have a unique masthead and matching footer. When having my graphic designers create a masthead and footer, I like to use colors similar to those on the client's website and/or logo. If you are not a graphic designer by trade, your masthead and footer need to be professionally created for you.

3. Name of newsletter

Typically you want the name to be something other than your business name unless your business name is descriptive of your service. For example, if you own West Village Dental, that shouldn't be the name of your newsletter. You may want to try something more along the lines of "The Monthly Smile." Our newsletter is called "The Newsletter Pro" because we are the premier newsletter company. We even have clients who get pretty creative with their newsletter names and use plays on words. We even have a client (this client happens to be a dentist) who loves his pets so much that part of his newsletter is written in the pets' voices. The dentist named his newsletter to reflect that. Get creative. Be fun! If you want to see an example of an article that his pets have written, I have included one in the business to consumer example section, at the end of the book.

Special Bonus!

If you haven't already done so, start right now by going to my website to receive a FREE 12-month premium print subscription to my monthly newsletter, plus a bonus copy of one of my Gold CDs titled "5 Ways to Use Newsletters to Increase Sales and Crush Your Competition." Both complement this book well. Just go to www.TheNewsletterpro.com/book and fill in the form on the screen. We'll mail (yes, a real physical hard copy of both the newsletter and CD will be mailed to you) the current month's newsletter and CD to you. Go to www.TheNewsletterpro.com/book. You will be happy you did!

4. Newsletter tagline

A tagline is a great place to highlight what makes you different. The reason a tagline is important is you never know who is going to end up with a copy of your newsletter and you want them to be able to quickly understand what it is that you do and what makes you special. Many times, you can use your company's unique selling proposition as the tagline. In case you are not familiar with a USP, here is a short definition below.

Business Nugget b

"A Unique Selling Proposition (USP) is a way of explaining your position against your competition. A USP is also a way of summarizing and telegraphing one of the chief benefits, often the chief benefit of the business, product, or service being marketed." —Dan Kennedy

5. Using pictures

As we talked about earlier, a picture is worth a thousand words, and you should use pictures as often as possible. One type of picture that is often over-looked is the personal picture. Whenever you have a chance, you should include a personal or family picture to help build that relationship with people. If you don't have that, what about your pet or your favorite vacation spot? Don't forget—you never know what is going to resonate with someone.

6. The length of your newsletter

A common question I get is how long should

a newsletter be. For 85% of people, a four-page newsletter is the preferred length. Some business models can justify an eight-page newsletter. Typically, I see people use an eight-page newsletter if they are selling B2B or membership-based products, or are a high-volume retailer. Like anything, there are exceptions to the rules, but most people will be fine with a four-page newsletter. Every now and again, I am asked about a two-page newsletter. In 99.6% of cases, a two-page newsletter is just too small because you can't get enough content on the page to make it valuable, as you will see in the next chapter where I lay out for you what type of content you should have in your newsletter. There is almost NO WAY you can include enough content in just two pages to make it as valuable as it needs to be. Because of the smaller size, you may even find yourself being tempted to only put in information about your business and industry so that you don't waste any valuable space. You will then quickly find yourself with a boring newsletter. For example, let's say you are a dentist who writes an article about tooth decay and root canals. Honestly, how many people are going to read that newsletter? I don't want to read that newsletter. Do you? One of the exceptions to creating a two-page newsletter is when you use the two-page newsletter as a supplement. For example, we have our main newsletter for "The Newsletter Pro" go out each month, and 15 days later, we have a second two-page newsletter, titled "The

Monthly Mullet," that we mail out. The job of "The Monthly Mullet" newsletter is to simply have some fun and be an additional touch with our clients and prospects.

CHAPTER 7
Email or Print Newsletters

This far into the book, I am sure it is obvious that I am a print newsletter guy, because I have mentioned the words "print newsletter" multiple times. But I didn't just come to that position without doing a little research, so here is what I found.

Email

Although email is "free" its deliverability rate is abysmal. The average mass commercial email (which your newsletter would be considered) by the major email players, like Google and Yahoo, only makes it to your prospects' inbox between 16% and 60% of the time. That is horrible. Of course, you won't know what percentage of your customers actually receive it or even who bothers to open and read it. If, for some reason, you want to reach only 16% to 60% of your clients this month, then maybe it is a good idea to do an e-newsletter. But, if you want to reach anywhere close to 100% of them, it is not going to happen with email.

A recent survey done by Marketing Sherpa found that the average read time on an email is between 15 and 20 seconds. WHAT!? You can't effectively build a relationship in 15 to 20 seconds a month. One of the reasons for such a fast readership rate is the infinite number of distractions that people have on the Internet. On their computers, they are only a click away from Facebook, ads, online video games, instant messages, and a bazillion other distractions. If all of that weren't bad enough, companies like Google have come up with new features like priority inbox where they sort your emails by what they think you will be more interested in reading. This means that every month your customers don't read your emails, they will be put into their inboxes in a lower and lower position. Eventually, if they never open them, they won't even make it into their inboxes. Now that sucks.

Print

The single biggest negative to a print newsletter is the cost. A print newsletter is going to cost more than an email newsletter. As far as other negatives go, it is harder to print a newsletter and keep up with postal regulations. Those are the negatives, as far as I see them.

We have covered many of the positives of a print newsletter in the book so far, but let's list out a few of the benefits you'll get with the print newsletter that you will NOT get with an email newsletter.

1. **Near 100% deliverability.** This by itself is worth the price of admission—your newsletter getting to EVERY client EVERY time!

2. **Staying power.** The average email hangs around for seconds; a newsletter can literally hang around for months. Remember when I told you the story of the franchise I was researching and ultimately bought? I still have a binder full of their old newsletters. They were that interesting and that fun to read!

3. **Brand building.** You can't build a brand if less than 60% of your emails are being delivered.

4. **Consumption.** Studies have shown the average person will NOT consume most email newsletters. On the other hand, they do consume most of a print newsletter.

5. **Pass-around value.** You may get your email newsletter forwarded, but in many instances, that forward is seen as spam. When I hand or mail you a print newsletter, you know it is not spam. You know that friends, family members, or neighbors

have read this publication and thought of you. They are giving it to you for a reason. That would make me read it. What about you?

6. **Increased referrals.** With readership of 15 to 20 seconds for the average email newsletter and less than 60% of people getting your newsletter, the average business sees no measurable increase in referrals from sending an email newsletter.

I could go on, but you get the point. Is an email newsletter better than nothing? Slightly, but it takes a massive amount of effort to publish a good newsletter each month. If you're going to invest all of that effort, you should get the maximum results.

A few days ago, I was sitting in a meeting with a lawyer, who said he knows how valuable his newsletter is but that he literally has to lock himself into a room for half a day to complete it. At his hourly rate, that is insane. But he knows the value of creating a good newsletter for his clients and referral sources, so he does it.

Still not sure whether print trumps email? On your spouse's next birthday, just send him or her an e-greeting card. Don't acknowledge his or her birthday in any other way. No real cards, no verbal acknowledgment, no gifts, no birthday nookie. Nothing but just an e-card. If that goes over well for you, then by all means send your newsletter via email.

CHAPTER 8
Creating Content for Your Newsletter

Universally, creating content is the single hardest part of publishing a monthly newsletter. Most people stare at a blank page and have a very hard time going from nothing to something. I fully understand. My company creates hundreds of unique newsletters, and even for our professional writers, it can be difficult at times. Below are some ideas for content and how to use them to help you go from a blank page to a finished newsletter.

Personal articles

Personal articles are the single most important element to having a successful newsletter, and they should be the easiest to write since they are about you, your life, your business, and your family. These articles represent the relationship-building aspect of your newsletter.

People struggle with these articles in three places:

1. People feel that their lives are boring and no one would care, but that couldn't be further from the truth. Most of us do something unique or exciting, or we have something unusual happen to us. Maybe you just got back from a vacation that was fun. We are all guilty of thinking our lives are boring and everyone else's lives are more exciting. Give your customers a bit of personal information, and you'll be surprised at how they connect with you and share similar personal stories from their lives.

2. The next place I see people struggle is with the idea of privacy. You don't need to share your innermost thoughts and secrets in the newsletter, but sharing information about your last vacation or talking about your love for NCAA football and how you enjoy the season tickets you have to watch every Boise State Broncos game (Go Broncos!) is not a breach of national security. That information is not really that personal. Likely, anyone who knows you even a little knows you're a huge fan. I have to be honest. I have struggled with this from time to time myself. The single most difficult and personal article I have ever put in my own

newsletter was titled "He Stopped Breathing for 3½ Minutes," accompanied by a picture of my almost three-year-old son, Jeremiah. I wrote the article a few days before his third birthday, and it tells the story of how he stopped breathing for three and a half minutes a few days before his first birthday. To be honest, when writing the story, it was so personal it made me start to tear up. I tried to write other articles for the newsletter, but I simply couldn't. He was what was on my mind that month. I published the article and had numerous people share similar experiences they had had or tell me they had teared up reading it. At the end of the day, some people may have read it and thought I was using my son, but that wasn't it at all. He and that situation were what was on my mind, and I decided to share the story. I have included a copy of this, plus two other examples of personal articles I have used in my newsletters, at the end of this chapter for you to read.

3. People struggle with giving enough information. When I review some of the newsletters we create for clients, I sometimes see personal articles that are two or three paragraphs long that don't really say much. Typically, when I see this, I go in and talk to our writers because for almost all of our customers, we interview them and then ghost write the articles. Our conversations go something like this:

Me: Why is this article so short?

Writer: The client was short on time this month and only gave me a little bit of information.

Me: Did you tell them this wasn't going to be enough information to write a full article and ask to reschedule?

Writer: Yup, they said it was OK if it was short this month.

But remember, these articles are SO important. Without these personal articles, it takes much longer to build those important relationships with your clients and prospects, and with some of them, they will never feel any connection with you without the personal article.

One of the primary goals of your newsletter is to let people get to know you so they feel connected to you. People do business with people they know and like. If you are not prepared to let people in, even if only a little bit, newsletters are likely not for you.

Fun pieces

All newsletters need an element of fun in them. These fun pieces can be in a mix of content and can change on a regular basis if you want. Below is a list of ideas of fun content you may want to include in your newsletter:

1. Sudoku puzzles
2. Crossword puzzles
3. Jokes
4. Funny pictures
5. Funny stories
6. Contests

Any combination of these will help increase readership and engagement with your newsletter. If you are still having issues figuring out what fun type of stuff people want to read, subscribe to Reader's Digest. Here are some other popular article types and ideas:

1. Top 10
2. Recipes
3. How to
4. Tips on parenting
5. Vacation ideas
6. Technology tips
7. Time management ideas
8. Luxury items

Both the fun section and these other articles would be considered nonrelevant content. This nonrelevant content is very important because it increases readership of the overall newsletter. Nothing is worse than sending a newsletter that no one reads. Not only have you wasted your money, but more importantly, you have wasted your time. Having a good mix of relevant content (content that is about your industry), nonrelevant content, and personal information is what is going to make your newsletter great.

* * *

Article from the July 2012 "The Newsletter Pro" – He Stopped Breathing for 3½ Minutes

On July 16, my son Jeremiah turned three years old. It was a day he had been looking forward to since my other son Tyler had turned six in January. Every year around Jeremiah's birthday, I take a moment and thank the Lord for another year with him because there was a time I wasn't sure he would live to see his first birthday—much less his third.

When Jeremiah was born, we knew right away that something was wrong with him. The gasping and grunting sounds he exerted while doing minor things we all take for granted (like breathing) were just not what you expect to hear from a brand new beautiful gift from God. As a parent, it is so very hard to see your kid sick or in pain. It is even harder to not know what is causing the problems.

After just under a year of struggling to find out what was wrong with Jeremiah, we were told he had severe sleep apnea. We scheduled an appointment to have a sleep study conducted. They hooked Jeremiah up to more probes and monitors than I thought they could physically fit on a baby (but they managed). These probes were monitoring everything—brain activity, the number of times he stopped breathing per hour, and everything in between. As they were hooking Jeremiah up, we noticed he had a slight fever and asked if that would affect the sleep study. The nurse told us it wouldn't, and they continued hooking him up.

The room at this sleep center is set up so the parents have one room and the baby has an adjoining room. My wife, Mariah, and I decided she would stay the night with Jeremiah so I could go home and be with our other kids. As the night went on and Mariah was just getting ready to doze off, she heard an alarming amount of noise coming from Jeremiah's room. She ran in to find him having a seizure. She screamed for the nurse, and the next thing she heard is every parent's worst nightmare—a droaning tone from the monitor, indicating that Jeremiah was flatlining.

They called 911 for an ambulance and tried to resuscitate him. As the monitor continued to go off, fear and panic set in, and time started to slow down. The feeling of helplessness was almost unbearable. After what felt to Mariah like an eternity, another minute ticked by. The monitors were still blaring, and the nurses continued to try to bring our baby boy back to life. Three minutes had passed, and still nothing. As a parent, you can only imagine the worst. You are literally begging God to save your child.

Finally, at three minutes and just over 30 seconds, baby Jeremiah took one shallow breath and then slowly another, and another. As he was loaded into the ambulance, Mariah (still in shock) called me and said, "Jeremiah had a seizure and stopped breathing for three and a half minutes. We are in an ambulance on our way to St. Al's downtown; I have to go" and hung up. I had NEVER moved so fast getting out of my house nor had I ever driven that fast down the freeway before. The whole time I did not know if my son was dead or alive. Tears were streaming down my cheeks, and I was praying that I hadn't lost him. I made it to the hospital to find that Jeremiah was in fact alive. There are no words to describe how relieved I was. He had numerous ER doctors all around him, and he was very disoriented, to say the least. I hugged and comforted my wife and waited for the doctors to finish.

We ultimately found out he had had a fibral seizure, which happens in about 20% of kids under five years old. The additional good news was that by the time he turned five, he would no longer be at risk for these seizures. We asked if he would experience any permanent damage from the three and a half minutes of not breathing or the seizure, and, thankfully, the answer was no. Brain damage doesn't set in until after four minutes of not breathing. Jeremiah ultimately had a few surgeries to fix the breathing issues and is now a happy and healthy three-year-old.

That day changed me both personally and professionally forever. As much as I enjoy working, and I do, I realized that on my death bed, I am not going to look back and say, "If I had only worked those few extra days, my life would be complete." In fact I believe it will be the opposite. I am much more likely to look back and say, "I should have spent more time with the people that mattered most to me."

I personally enjoy working and really don't see a day even in my distant future where I won't work at least a little, but it is important to find a good balance and make sure that every day you take a little time for those people in your life who really matter. At the end of this life, nothing else is going to seem more important.

Shaun Buck

P.S. Do me a favor. When you get home today, kiss all the little (or big) Jeremiahs that you have running around.

Article from the September 2012 "The Newsletter Pro" – I'm an Idiot and I Can Prove It

Like many entrepreneurs over the years, I have had times where I've done very well for myself, making a good to very good six-figure income. Also, like many entrepreneurs, I have had times where I've been broke, struggling to make payroll and pay the bills. A number of years back, while I was trying to grow one of my companies, I was struggling, not with payroll or paying the bills, because we were doing well, but with something far worse. You see, what I didn't realize was those hard times where I had been broke in the past messed with my head. They made me fearful of being broke again so, in turn, I was pinching pennies (or as my wife would say, I was being cheap). I also developed a nasty disease called NOCDIAGAM (aka No One Can Do It As Good As Me) during that period of my life. NOCDIAGAM is a wicked sickness that literally sucks the life out of you, as it compels you to have to do everything yourself, and (as any good business person knows) in business, you can't get very far doing everything yourself.

At the time due to my cheapness in almost all areas of my business and my NOCDIAGAM disease, my business was just treading water. Even though personally I was working very hard, both in the business and on the business, I wasn't seeing any growth. A few years ago, a very smart woman (my wife, Mariah) pointed out to me that I was an idiot. Of course, she didn't use the word "idiot." Instead, she started asking me questions about why I was being so cheap. She asked me to explain how I justified pinching pennies in every aspect of my life (when I knew that we had plenty of money) and why I felt I needed to do everything myself. Being the loving wife that she is, she led me to the obvious conclusion that I was acting like a fool and I simply was NOT ever going to achieve my goals living life with that philosophy.

I identified four areas that were holding me back and worked on each one to overcome them.

1. **Being too cheap.** I once heard someone say, you can never make $100,000 per year doing $10.00 per hour work. But many business owners give it a shot. If your time is worth $100.00 per hour, you need to do everything in your power to be working on $100.00 per hour work, not $10.00 per hour work.

2. **No one can do it as good as me.** I eventually realized this was simply ridiculous. The reason I didn't think anyone could do it as good as me was because I was hiring the wrong people. Once I created a training system and started hiring the right people, not only did I find people who could do it as well as me, I found people who were better than I was.

3. **Lack of investment in my business.** Because I was cheap, I would save every penny I could for a rainy day. Of course, I still save, but now I also put aside money for investing in my business. Recently, I invested in new equipment to allow us to increase production, as well as new marketing systems that bring leads in on auto pilot. Of course, neither is cheap, nor are they easy, but my return on investment for both has been and likely

will continue to be tremendous.

4. **The bad news diet.** I used to spend an hour or two a day watching or reading the news. It is impossible to pick up a paper or watch the news without thinking the sky is falling, even when it is not falling around you. It was making me slightly depressed. I have gone to a strict no more than 10 minutes per day bad news diet, and let me tell you, it has done wonders for my outlook on life and business.

Where in your life are you making decisions or reacting from fear? Are you stepping over dollars to get to dimes by doing $10.00 per hour work? Are you scared of investing in your business? After getting slapped in the face by my wife (figuratively speaking, of course), taking a hard look in the mirror, and working to make tough changes in my business and personal life, I can honestly say I am a better husband, father, and business owner. If this story resonates with you in anyway, feel free to consider this your figurative slap in the face.

Article from the March 2013 "The Newsletter Pro" – Know Your Numbers, and I Don't Mean Your Batting Average

I just got back from a small conference in Orlando, Florida, where one of my companies, The Newsletter Pro, was an exhibitor. We have never exhibited before, and I really didn't know what to expect in the way of sales. What I did know was that between booth space, airfare, hotel, and marketing material for the booth, I was into this show close to $5,000 dollars. To justify spending 5,000 bucks for this test, I really needed to make sure I signed up at least five new clients. But with no experience exhibiting, I didn't know if my expectation of five new clients was realistic or not. Ultimately that left me with a decision. Do I test exhibiting and risk losing up to $5,000 but possibly gain a new way to grow my company, or do I do nothing, keep my 5,000 dollars, but guarantee that I will never know if exhibiting is a viable way to market The Newsletter Pro?

This exact dilemma faces business owners all over the country on a daily basis. Unfortunately, most of them have no clue if the marketing they are about to test will work or not because most of them don't even know their numbers so they can begin to figure out if this type of marketing works. If you've ever watched the ABC show the Shark Tank (and if you are not watching it, you should be), you'll notice the cardinal sin when a business owner is asking for an investment from the sharks is not knowing your numbers. It virtually guarantees they won't be getting an investment from any of the sharks.

Here are a few of the most important numbers all business owners need to know about their businesses but most don't know:

1. What is your monthly break-even number?

2. How much is the average new client/patient worth to you over the next 12 months?

3. What is the average lifetime value of a new client/patient to your company?

4. How much are you willing to spend to get a new client/patient in the front door?

5. How many new clients/patients do you need to meet your sales goals for the quarter/year?

This is just the tip of the iceberg when it comes to knowing your numbers, but I can tell you that I can stump 97% of business owners I meet with before the fourth question. How can you make a decision to invest in marketing or anything else for that matter if you don't know these numbers?

A few years ago, I didn't know my numbers, and back then I never would have risked $5,000 on a marketing campaign that may or may not have worked. But today, I know that on average, if I sign up one new newsletter or direct mail client, I could have at least broken even on the $5,000 investment over the lifetime value of that client, not including any referrals I would get from my new client. (Which is another good number to know.) So in the end, I felt the risk for me and the company was minimal, but it was only minimal because I know my numbers. Do you know yours?

Note: In the past, I would have stopped an article at the previous period, or question mark in this case, which would have left you wondering how I did with exhibiting. I would have done this for the same reason any marketing company would have, and that is because, as an industry, we tend to want to share only the times when we knock it out of the park. But the reality is that no business knocks it out of the park 100% of the time. To stick with the baseball analogy, this time we got a double. We signed up three new clients at the event and ended up with two dozen or so leads, of which we hope will lead to at least two additional clients so that we reach our goal of five new clients.

We may or may not end up with any additional clients no matter what. I will more than break even over time, and I now have a working knowledge of running an exhibit, as well as ideas to make our next, much bigger exhibiting event in May even better. Plus, I will have the opportunity to test our follow-up sequence on the leads we receive before the event in May. This is how great marketing

Business Nugget 9
To see other examples of content published in my newsletter and newsletters we have created for clients, please check out the last few chapters of the book.

comes about with any media. You test something new, make minor changes, and simply rinse and repeat. I hope giving you a behind-the-curtain look at some inside baseball (I know I may have taken the baseball thing a bit too far) will be helpful for you. I know it has helped me in the past.

CHAPTER 9
The Top 6 Mistakes People Make When Publishing Their Newsletter

I get to see a ton of self-published newsletters. Because of that, I have seen more than a few mistakes. Below is a list of the top 6 mistakes I see most often with self-published newsletters. I decided to put these in order of how detrimental the mistake is to achieving the goals we looked at previously in the book.

Mistake Number 1 – Not Publishing Monthly

This is by far the single biggest mistake people make. When you don't publish monthly, you lose most of the benefits you get from publishing a newsletter.

Let me give you some examples. One of the benefits you are trying to achieve with your newsletter is building a relationship. How much of a relationship can you build if you are talking to your customers only every few months? The answer is no relationship. When you mail only every few months, people can't remember the last time they got one or whether they even liked it the last time they got it. Heck, they may not even remember who you are, let alone feel they have any relationship with you.

Think about it like this: How often do you communicate with people you like and have a relationship with? Of course, some people you talk to more often and others less often, but few people have a real relationship with others that they talk to only every few months. Let me give you an example. If I have not talked to my dad on the phone in more than four or five days, I may get a voicemail from him asking me whether everything is OK. Our relationship is such that, even if he has not heard from me in a relatively short time frame like four or five days, he starts to wonder whether everything is OK. On the other hand, I have some "friends," who truly used to be friends a decade ago, whom I speak with only every three to 12 months. At this point, we aren't really friends anymore. Typically, when one of us calls, it is because we need something or are bored waiting for a plane or driving some long distance and we have run out of other people to call and things to do. There is no relationship there. We have some familiarity, but we don't have a relationship.

What kind of relationship do you want to have with your customers, referral sources, and prospects? If your customers aren't very important to you and you don't want more referrals, by all means send quarterly. Otherwise, you have to send monthly. Keep that close relationship with them.

Note: I know I was laying it on a bit thick in the last paragraph. I also know your customers are important to you. Without them, you wouldn't be in business. Of course, I understand that. The reason I laid it on so thick was because I see too many people take their customers for granted and then wonder why business is down or patients don't take recommended treatments. I know it can be scary at first mailing monthly, but it is the only way to get the results you want and need.

Mistake Number 2 – Being Boring

I see boring newsletters a lot. All industries publish them, but the one I get at my house happens to be a dental newsletter. Each month, this stock newsletter talks all about gum disease and teeth. I cringe every time it comes in the mail. The last thing in the world I would ever want to read is a newsletter about gum disease. And to add insult to injury, they include pictures in this newsletter. Seriously, no one, not even dental students, want to read about or see pictures of someone's rotting gums. The funny thing is that some 60% to 70% of Americans have at least a minor fear of the dentist. Who in their right mind thought it would be a good idea to mail a monthly newsletter about dental horrors where 60% to 70% of the people who would get the newsletter have at least a mild fear about dentistry? That would be like Delta airlines sending a monthly newsletter all about airplane crashes and close calls to people who are scared of flying. It is just nuts. Not to mention the fact that NO one is reading it. My estimates are that boring newsletters have less than a 10% readership rate and less than a 2% cover-to-cover readership. What a waste of time and money! If you are a dentist mailing a newsletter like this, STOP IT!

Note: I know my estimates are not scientific, but they are based on a survey I did on readership of a boring newsletter.

The moral of the story is, don't mail a boring newsletter just for the sake of mailing a newsletter. I guess there is really a second moral to the story, which is, don't mail a newsletter that will scare people. That simply isn't good business in most cases.

At the end of the day, it is far more fun and profitable to take half of the money you would have spent on creating, printing, and mailing your boring newsletter and simply light that money on fire. After that, you can take the other half of the money and have a fun night on the town. You will get more bang for your buck doing that than you will sending out a boring newsletter. :)

Mistake Number 3 – Not Mailing to the Whole List

I am surprised by how often people want to know whom to mail to. To me, the answer to this question is obvious:

1. Anyone you want to do more business with in the future

2. Anyone you want to send you a referral

3. Anyone who has expressed an interest in your business but has not yet bought from you

When you look at that list, who would you want to cut out? But I see people cut people from that list all the time.

The most undermailed to person on the above list is the person who has not yet bought something from you. As I shared with you at the start of this book, this is the one person you for sure want to mail to on a regular basis. That's how the dry cleaning franchisee sold me on buying a franchise, and if you follow up with your prospects, you will also close more deals. Let me share another story with you. Just recently I had a guy call whom I had met five months ago and say he was ready to work with us to get his monthly newsletter out. He actually thanked me for mailing my newsletter to him each month and said it had been a goal of his to get his monthly newsletter out and that, if I had not mailed my newsletter to him each month, he never would have remembered who we were so he could get help.

When we meet prospective clients, we put them on our mailing list for a minimum of one year. I have found that people are ready to buy when they are ready to buy, and for the most part, you are not going to rush them into a buying decision. But if you have kept in touch them, when they are ready to buy, they are not going to think of all of your competitors whom they haven't heard from; they are going to think of you, the person who has been following up with them for months.

If you have a group of people who naturally should be referring to you, they need to get a monthly newsletter from you. Here are some examples of natural referral sources:

- Personal injury attorneys can get referrals from chiropractors.
- Oral surgeons can get referrals from general dentists.
- Estate and trust lawyers can get referrals from accountants.

Even if a company has never sent you a referral,

you can add them to your newsletter list cold, and over time some of those cold leads will start sending you referrals. At the beginning of the year, one of our personal injury attorneys told me that, since he had started mailing his newsletter cold to chiropractors in his area, the number of referrals he has gotten from them has doubled. Not too bad if you ask me.

Finally comes the idea of mailing to anyone you want to do business with in the future. This is where the list could get really big. As a rule of thumb, if people haven't done business with you within the past 12 to 24 months, they likely shouldn't be on this list. Of course, some businesses with a very high average customer lifetime value (LTV) may mail longer and some with lower LTV may mail for a shorter period of time, but as a general rule 12 to 24 months works.

Mistake Number 4 – Poor Design

I have seen newsletters published by large companies that appear to have been designed by the boss's eight-year-old on Microsoft Paint. Your newsletter should match the image you are trying to convey. If your image is we are a very small mom and pop company, by all means do it yourself. If your image is that you are a professional company, your newsletter also needs to look professional. You wouldn't meet new clients and hand them the free business cards you can get from VistaPrint.com that have an ad for

VistaPrint.com on the back of them, would you? What about handing out business cards that are printed from your home inkjet printer and have the perforated edges that scream, I printed these at home and have no money? Are you going to hand those out? Of course not. So don't create a newsletter that looks the same way. Unless you are a graphic designer and have been paid to do graphic design work by more than a dozen people in the past, don't try to lay out your own newsletter.

Mistake Number 5 – Giving Up Too Soon!

Newsletters are not a get-rich-quick scheme. They are not going to make customers flood through your front door on the first issue. In reality, it takes somewhere between four and nine months for your business to realize all of the benefits a newsletter provides. Before you go into publishing a newsletter, you need to understand it takes time to build readership, it takes time to build that relationship, it takes time to see results. Of course, I can tell you stories of people who have seen massive results much sooner, but don't go in banking on massive results from day one, because you will be disappointed. You should think of your newsletter as a long-term investment, not a quick flip for a profit. That's the truth.

Mistake Number 6 – Allowing Other People to Advertise in Your Newsletter

I have never understood the idea of allowing other people to put a blatant ad in your newsletter. To be honest, this isn't a mistake I see as often as the other five mistakes, but I am always baffled when I do. Ads for other people's products and services as a rule should not be allowed. If you are going to violate the sanctity of your newsletter, at least do it for your own benefit.

From time to time, I do allow people to post guest articles or a resource box or even a small offer. But that is as far as I personally will go. If there is a time that you feel you need to allow an ad in your newsletter, the advertiser needs to follow the same rules you do and place the ad as a freestanding insert (FSI).

CHAPTER 10
5 Ways to Use a Newsletter to Grow Your Business

Idea Number 1 – Cold mail your newsletter.

This idea is by no means new or unique to me, but it works. Find a list of people who are ideal for your product or service, and add each and every one of them to your monthly newsletter. We have seen this work in a number of industries. One of my favorite stories is one of a realtor we mail for. She sends a very fun and interesting newsletter to every homeowner in the neighborhoods for which she would like to be the realtor of choice. The average price of a home in the very first neighborhoods she used this strategy with is between $250,000 and $300,000. On her third mailing, she listed not one but two houses.

The commission for those two houses will be more than enough money to cover her newsletter mailing to that neighborhood for years to come. And another bonus—she is now seen as the choice realtor for that neighborhood.

As I mentioned earlier, if you have a group of people who would make great referral sources, they should all be getting a newsletter from you. If you are going to be sending to a large group of people, for example, a personal injury attorney who is mailing to all the chiropractors in his area, then you want to have a separate newsletter just for them. In the chiropractors' newsletter you are going to create, you should have all of the elements we talked about earlier, for example, a personal article and some fun content. But in the sections where you may have put an interesting nonrelevant article, you should instead insert information that will help your clients and / or prospects grow their business or improve their practice or quality of life. Since you are mailing to referral sources, you can typically afford to spend more per piece that is mailed out because you will be able to see direct business typically much sooner from this type of newsletter. We have found that the addition of a monthly CD that helps the chiropractors in this example grow their business will increase the number of doctors who refer to you because of your mailing, as well as the number of referrals each doctor gives you. Another great addition is a staff newsletter. This

Business Nugget 10
Sometimes you will need a list to get all the names and addresses of people you want to cold mail to. A good source for lists is www.NextMark.com. One word of caution: Most of their lists are one-time use only, so make sure you check on how many times you can mail the list so you don't run afoul of the list broker.

newsletter should help them do their jobs better, and it should have a ton of fun and interesting content in it.

Cold newsletter mailing is a great way to generate new leads and business from your newsletter. Whom can you cold mail a newsletter to who can refer new business to your company?

Idea Number 2 – Distribute copies of your newsletter to other businesses that have similar customers and/or waiting rooms.

This is a pretty simple idea but also very effective if you have local businesses that your ideal client is at. Go talk to the business owner, and ask whether you can leave copies of your newsletter for his customers to read. If your ideal clients are sitting in waiting rooms, this is a no-brainer for both you and the business owners because they get free content that helps keep their customers entertained. If they don't have a waiting room, ask whether you can leave a small stand and free copies of your newsletter near the cash register where their customers check out or someplace else that makes sense.

When you use this strategy, it is a good idea to have some kind of lead generation call to action in the newsletter. For example, offer a free report with the top 7 things that you must know before you buy a new car. This way the newsletter doesn't come across to business owners as just another advertisement. Business owners will be more inclined to allow you to put the newsletter in their place of business if it isn't chock full of coupons. We have clients who put out newsletters with a coupon or two, and that is OK for some businesses. But by far, most companies will be better served by putting the lead-generation piece instead of the coupon in the newsletter.

Business Nugget 11

When you distribute these newsletters, make sure you do NOT personally deliver them. As a business owner, unless you are stopping by a top referral source or a client's office, that is a complete waste of time. You should have no problem finding someone who will run all over town for eight bucks an hour and a full tank of gas.

A great example of a company that has created a whole franchise system from placing newsletters in businesses that are high traffic is Coffee News®. They place good news newsletters in businesses and sell ad space in the newsletters. As of 2012, they have 576 franchisees in the United States and 945 worldwide. Now personally, I think the advertising in these newsletters is awful. But the idea is excellent, and if done properly, it can work well for you too.

Idea Number 3 – Mail to prospects and include an offer.

This one is a no-brainer. When you are mailing to your prospects, from time to time, include an offer for your product or service. Make it a newsletter-only offer, one they can't get anywhere else. Even better, make it an irresistible offer. Try to convert some of these prospects into customers.

My preferred method of making the offer is via a freestanding insert (FSI). The FSI can be all advertising. You don't need to include any real content, but you still need to preserve the sanctity of the newsletter.

Another great way to use an FSI in a newsletter is for list segmentation. List segmentation is a book in and of itself, but you can put offers for free reports, white papers, CDs, etc. And based on the topic of the report you are giving away, segment your list so you know who is most interested in what. For example, if you are a dentist and you put an offer on an FSI for a report on veneers and 11 patients opt in to get that free report, wouldn't it be a good idea to send them some additional information on veneers, maybe even make them an offer? A veneer patient can spend from $15,000 to $25,000. If you knew 11 people from your practice were very interested in veneers, could you afford to spend $200 on each of those people to get one or two of them to pull the trigger and spend $15,000 to $25,000? Of course you could. Using an FSI to segment your list so you can make direct offers to people who are interested in specific products and services you offer is smart business.

Idea Number 4 – Use your newsletter as another touch mechanism within a direct mail campaign.

When you are mailing a direct mail campaign, time permitting, I have seen a huge increase in response when a newsletter is also mailed out separately to

Business Nugget 12

My personal preference is to use this step between steps two and three of your direct mail campaign. I have found this works the best. Of course, with any direct mail tip, the only way to know for sure is to test it out for yourself and track the results.

the prospect. Some people simply send their standard monthly newsletter, and others create a special newsletter that is a really well-disguised sales piece. However you choose to do it, you can see a nice bump in response rate by adding a newsletter step into the middle of a direct mail campaign.

Idea Number 5 – Reactivate former customers.

According to the Rockefeller Corporation, 68% of consumers leave a business because they think the business doesn't care about them! Seriously think about that for a second—68% of people leave a company because they think the company doesn't care about them. If perception is reality, then at least 68% of the people who have ever done business with you think you don't care. That's crazy, right? Of course you care. These are the people who allow you to keep your doors open and the lights on. These customers are the ones who allow you to pay your employees and feed your kids—literally. How can it be that they feel you don't care? Have you ever heard the saying actions speak louder than words? They feel this way because you don't show them you care. It's funny. Sometimes a company will try to show they care by sending an email thank-you or a greeting card. Are you kidding me? In my mind, that is almost worse than doing nothing at all. It is kind of like saying we care but not enough to spend any money on you, so we are just going to email it. Another way to think about it is if you have ever been on Facebook on your birthday and you see all these people wishing you a happy birthday. Come on. Do those people really care about you? Of course they don't. Facebook told them it was your birthday, or they saw everyone else posting Happy Birthday and decided to join in on the fun. In the end, it is meaningless.

By sending your newsletter to people who have not bought your product or used your service recently but are now considered inactive, you can and will reactivate many of them. For the 68% who have left because they felt you didn't care, showing them that you do care will go a long way to winning them back.

I recently heard a story from a caterer who sent his newsletter to clients who had not done  *Business Nugget 13* *A reactivatied previous customer is the third easiest type of person to sell to.* business with him as far back as three years previously. After the first issue, those inactive clients produced $6,000 in new orders. Had he never sent the newsletter, those people would still be lost, and he would have almost NO chance of getting other additional business or referrals from them. As he continues to mail his newsletter to these lost customers, he will see more and more of them coming back.

CHAPTER 11
Become a Good Pointer

A few years ago, I was awful at outsourcing and, even to some extent, at hiring employees to do tasks I could do myself. The reason I had this problem always seemed to come down to one of two issues.

1. I felt I could do "it" better than anyone else.

2. I was being cheap and didn't want to make an investment in my business.

What I found was that by trying to do everything myself and not investing in my business, my business plateaued. What I didn't realize at the time was that when you try to do everything yourself, inevitably you end up doing things that you're not good at, but also you end up doing many things you simply don't like and would prefer not to do. This causes all kinds of problems when trying to grow a business. I knew intellectually that I shouldn't be doing $8.00 an hour work. Also, intellectually, I knew that there were many people who could do the job better than I could, but for some reason I couldn't let go. Some of the reasons I struggled with letting go of tasks was partially due to a scarcity mindset I had at the time. A funny thing happened, though. I started to let go as I started to hire out tasks that I really wasn't good at and frankly didn't want to do. Almost immediately, I started to achieve more success in my business. Sales grew, profits went up, I attracted more clients because the work I outsourced was being done better, work even stopped feeling like work (most of the time at least), and finally, I was happier than ever before. It is very important to focus on the few things in your business that you enjoy and that you are good at, and let others do the rest for you. The same goes for your newsletter as well. Below is a reprint of an article I wrote that details the system I use to get stuff off of my plate and grow my business bigger, better, and faster.

Point Your Way to More Fun and Profits!

At the end of each year, I do two things religiously:

1. I work on my marketing calendar and my plan for my businesses for the upcoming year.

2. I reflect on areas where I didn't accomplish my goals for the previous year and try to pinpoint items I am currently doing in my business that quite simply, I don't find enjoyable.

Nearly every business owner knows she should have a business plan and a marketing calendar, so I don't want to focus on those activities in this article. What I want to look at is point number two—reflecting on areas in my business and life where I did not achieve my goals and the things that I'd prefer not to be doing in my business anymore. These two areas are more tied together than most people realize. In fact, I bet if you were to make a list (like I do) of things you weren't able to accomplish and the things you don't like doing, you will find that most of them are one in the same. If you don't like doing a certain type of project or task, you are far more likely to procrastinate in getting it done, which in turn means you don't complete all of your plans and goals for the year. It's a vicious cycle.

I have found that there is one surefire way to break this cycle of planning, procrastinating, and simply not getting your tasks done—become a better "pointer."

I believe I actually first heard the phrase being a good pointer from speaker and author Lee Milteer. Being a good pointer was described to me as being able to recognize the tasks and activities you are good at, as well as enjoy doing, and focus as much of your time as possible on those areas of your business. Now you take everything that is left (the stuff you don't want to do), and you simply "point," or instruct your employee, outsourcers, or other companies to do the "not so fun tasks" for you. Instantly you'll become happier and more productive because you are focusing on tasks you not only enjoy doing but you are likely good at to boot.

Let me pull it all together with five easy steps you can take to implement this in your business right now.

Step 1: Review any goals (written or otherwise) that have been around for so long now they are starting to feel like a pet.

Step 2: Create a list of tasks that would need to be accomplished to get those goals completed and off your list.

Step 3: Make a list of tasks you currently do in your business that you wish were no longer your responsibility.

Step 4: Look at the lists from steps 2 and 3. Any tasks that are on both lists need to be assigned to another person/vendor. It is OK if you don't know who that is yet. If you see another task on the list from step 2 that someone else would be better suited to accomplish, go ahead and assign that as well.

Step 5: Assign yourself the remaining tasks on the list from step 2 (these should mostly be tasks you enjoy and are good at).

Really that is all there is to it. I know it sounds simple. You may even think it sounds too simple, but just because it is simple doesn't mean it won't work.

CHAPTER 12
Business-To-Business Sample Articles

"The Newsletter Pro" July 2012 – What Happens When Prospects Don't Buy?

When you offer a good product or service, it can be very frustrating when people don't buy from you. It can be especially frustrating when they don't buy and you invested time, money, and effort to get them interested in your business. So, in this article, I want to look at the four choices prospects have when they choose not to buy immediately and how you can use this information to your advantage.

1. **They can do nothing.** Doing nothing is by far the easiest action for most people to take and is also the most common action taken after the average prospect chooses not to buy.

2. **Delay buying.** People choose to delay a purchase for a variety of reasons, the most common being financial in nature (i.e., not enough money right now, want to price shop, etc.).

3. **They buy from a competitor.** We all know this happens, and we all have had it happen to us. It can happen because of price comparison or other simple causes, but sometimes it happens because a competitor asked for the sale and nobody from your company ever did.

4. **They buy a different solution.** If they choose this, it typically means your product or service didn't meet their needs. Or they simply didn't understand enough about your product or service to know that it really did meet their needs.

Reasons number one and two are the most common of the four reasons people don't buy. These also happen to be the areas that are easiest to impact in your business, so I am going to focus on those reasons for not buying.

When prospects choose to do nothing, they are choosing to live with the problem they initially wanted solved rather than accepting your service. If a dentist recommends an extensive debridement cleaning to avoid eventual loss of teeth or worse, you might expect people to break open their wallets and pay for the extensive cleaning. Let me assure you, that doesn't always happen. But, just because it doesn't happen right on the spot, doesn't mean patients don't want to buy. They just weren't ready to buy at that moment. Of course, patients tell themselves they will come back, but rarely do they. Newton's first law of motion states that an object at rest tends to stay at rest unless an external force is applied to it. The same is true for prospects who don't buy. In the case of most businesses and dental practices, there is no mechanism in place that can apply this external force (e.g., multiple letters, phone calls, newsletters, etc.) and, in turn, patients simply don't come back. To add insult to injury, many of these patients who never acted also simply stop coming to the practice altogether because they're embarrassed that they did nothing.

The second reason people don't buy is that they delay the buying decision for one reason or another, although many of the reasons they are delaying are financial in nature. To overcome this reason NOT to buy, it helps to have some kind of sense of urgency (e.g., limited quantity, limited time, sale price, etc.). If the reason they are delaying the purchase is purely financial, a sense of urgency can help them to break out the old credit card and pay in full. But another way to encourage them to make a decision is to offer additional payment options. These options could be in-house credit, equal monthly payments via a credit or debit card, or a monthly membership that gets them what they want now. To see a really good example of the membership option, look at Banfield

Pet Hospital and check out their pet Optimum Wellness Plans®. Even if you don't run a veterinary clinic, it is a great model to follow.

By simply focusing on these four reasons prospects don't buy, and creating systems and processes to follow up and overcome objections, you will see huge increases to your bottom line. As an added bonus, by solving these problems, all of the investments you are making in marketing will yield a better return since you will be closing more sales from all of your leads.

"The Newsletter Pro" October 2012 – The Top 5 Reasons Your Business Should Have a Stellar Marketing Plan

Marketing your business today is a whole different game from what it was five or 10 years ago. With social media sites, blogs, and other shiny new marketing concepts coming out every day, it is an exciting time to be in the marketing business. The problem with all this thrilling new growth is that it can make your business's marketing seem sporadic. The temptation to move on to the latest and greatest can make it so that many of your marketing tasks never actually get seen through to the end, and you can basically end up expending a lot of energy and seeing very few results. So what is the best way to be sure that you are doing the best, most effective marketing for your business? Simple. Have a kick-butt strategic marketing plan!

1. Keep your marketing efforts proactive.

If you are wondering why you need a set marketing plan, why you can't just take ideas as they come and run with them, look no further than the growth you want to see in your business for your answer. As you likely know, in business, if you aren't growing, you are dying. And even if your business isn't struggling, sitting at status quo for too long can be dangerous. A smart marketing plan keeps your company's efforts proactive and ensures that you have a clearly set plan of "attack" to help you build and grow your business. A plan will protect your organization against the temptation of impulse marketing (reacting to every new technology, marketing platform, or other opportunities) and help you define and execute strategies in a way that helps you not only ensure the growth of your company but also have a measurable way to track your progress.

2. A plan helps you keep the big picture in mind.

A marketing plan helps you, your staff, and everyone else involved in your company see exactly what your company is working toward and how. It clearly lays out what your company's goals for the next quarter or year are and helps everyone understand how those goals are going to be met. A good plan will help you and your company keep sight of the big picture so you don't get lost in the weeds and you don't miss out on opportunities.

3. A marketing plan measures your progress.

Think of your marketing plan as the blueprint to help you track your marketing efforts. Use a tool like Base-camp or another online project management facilitator to help you see exactly what's being done when and by whom. This allows you to see what's working and what isn't. That way, if there is a bottle neck in your company (a certain area where things just aren't getting done or that is struggling), it will allow you to address the issue and fix it before you stray too far off your task time line.

4. A solid plan makes it easier to evaluate new opportunities.

So before, when I said not to fall into the trap of the "new and shiny," that isn't to say that all new ideas and technology are bad. It's just that if you get too caught up in staying "current," you often get off task from what your original goal was. When you already have a stable marketing plan in place, with clearly defined strategies and goals, it is easy to take a new idea as it comes along and evaluate how it would fit in with your current plan. If it is something that is easily integrated and would benefit the plan, then, great, include it. But if by trying to work on some new marketing toy you would end up putting the bulk of your efforts on hold for a while, you would be able to see that before you waste valuable time implementing something that isn't right for your company.

5. A plan gives you confidence.

All companies have ups and downs. When you are up, you feel invincible, but when you are down, it is easy to feel like things will never get better. The best way to pull you and your company out of one of these slumps is, yep, you guessed it—a great marketing plan! Sometimes just the simple act of getting some aggressive ideas down on paper can be enough to get your bottom line headed in the right direction. A good plan will guide you through the bad times and help you stay on track during the good times. It will confirm your direction, provide insight into your situation, and remind you of where you're heading. It will give you the confidence to stay strong when things seem tough.

There are several other reasons that a marketing plan can benefit you, but we only had room to list a few here. If you need help getting a stellar plan in place, reach out to us! We would be more than happy to help you map out a plan to help take your business to the next level of success.

"The Newsletter Pro" November 2012 – 5 Surefire Steps to Magically Predict Sales and Grow Your Business

Wouldn't it be great if you could predict the amount of sales your business was going to have this week, next week, or even next quarter, with a reasonable amount of accuracy?

How would that change your business, or even your life?

Being able to predict your future sales would allow you to foresee a potential slump in profits and plan additional marketing to increase sales. Or maybe you could set aside some extra cash from a more profitable quarter to help out with cash flow during a slow period. If you knew you were going to be busy, you could make sure you had the appropriate staff available to serve all your customers. Wouldn't being able to predict future sales be a game changer for you and your business?

Unfortunately, for most small businesses, the idea of being able to predict the future sounds much more like fantasy than reality. But it doesn't have to be. Prediction of future sales happens all the time on Wall Street, and if they can predict future sales in huge Fortune 500 companies, then we should be able to do it on Main Street.

Here are the 5 steps to being able to predict your future sales and grow your business:

Step 1 – You must build a list of current customers, prospects, and inactive customers. It is next to impossible for a small business to predict future sales without a list. For most businesses, their single biggest asset is their list and the relationship they have with their list. When building your list, the more contact info you can get, the better quality list you will have.

Step 2 – You need to track everything in your business, from the number of customers through the door on Tuesdays to the frequency and size of purchases your customers make. You have to track all of your marketing and analyze the data. Knowledge is power, and when you keep track of this kind of data, you will be able to find areas that you are doing well in, areas that need improvement, and even opportunities you may be missing. But if you aren't taking the time to track the data, then you can't reap the benefits. So make it a priority!

Step 3 – Once you have laid the foundation with the first two steps, it is time to create a marketing plan. At a minimum, your marketing plan should include the following:

1. A detailed quarterly marketing strategy with each marketing activity broken down to the day you plan on mailing, calling, texting, or sky writing (or whatever your company prefers) to your customers and prospects. Make sure you take into account holidays or other traditionally slow times in your business.

2. A few backup marketing ideas in case your tracking shows that one of your marketing campaigns is not performing up to par.

3. Your company's customer reactivation campaign

and schedule.

4. Your company's customer relationship-building and retention campaign and schedule.

5. Finally, you need to assign responsibility for creation and completion of all the marketing tasks.

Step 4 – Create your sales goals. With all of your newfound information and your marketing plan, you will be able to start making more accurate sales goals that are based on facts and not just hopes and dreams. The way I create sales goals for my company is by starting with projections of what current regular customers are going to be spending, adding in one-off sales estimates, and finally, looking at my marketing plan and estimating the number of new clients we should get from each piece of marketing we have planned for the month.

One thing you might try is working toward your sales goal on a rewards basis. When I set a quarterly goal, I divide that into smaller monthly goals, and when I hit any of my goals, I always have a reward for myself or my staff (something fun that we wouldn't normally do or buy) as an additional motivation for working toward the goal.

Step 5 – Work and rework your plan. As with learning anything new, you are going to struggle with all of this planning and goal setting at first, but it truly is the difference for many between success and failure.

You need to learn to run your business, not have your business run you.

By combining these five steps and creating a killer marketing plan, you will not only grow sales, but you too will be able to predict growth and sales like a Wall Street pro.

"The Newsletter Pro" January 2013 – The One Thing You MUST Do for Your Business in 2013

Do you remember 10 to 15 years ago when the "right" thing to do was write a business plan that was supposed to guide your business for three to five years or more? I don't know about you, but my business is moving so fast that any business plan I write will be obsolete in six months. So I don't recommend a traditional business plan, but a clear marketing calendar that is good for the next six to 12 months is a must if you want to see serious growth over the next 12 months. Writing your marketing calendar doesn't have to be complicated. There are four simple steps you must take.

Step 1 – You need to brainstorm every possible way to market. There are no good or bad ideas. You simply want to brain dump every possible idea onto a piece of paper. You can filter out the crap ones later. You may want to seek help from a competent business-minded person to make sure you don't miss anything. Typically, this person should be someone who is either very knowledgeable in marketing or more successful than you are. You may have heard the saying don't take money advise from broke people. The same goes for marketing advise—don't take it from someone whose business sucks.

Step 2 – Organize your ideas. Know that you have all your ideas in one place. Take a moment to evaluate each idea and organize them into categories. Some of the categories I use are as follows:

- Outrageous
- Quick to implement
- Bad ideas
- Ideas others can do for me
- Good ideas
- Ideas that need more research

Now you can discard the bad ideas and do a bit more research on the ideas that need more. Once you are done with your research, discard any additional bad ideas, and put the other ideas into the appropriate categories.

Step 3 – Once you have all of your ideas, you need to make a list of all of the steps you will need to take to implement each idea. It is OK if some of the steps say something to the extent of hire ABC company. If you have employees, you can note that you will be assigning an employee to complete the steps. I have found at times that this step can be a bit tedious, but it is very important not to skip over this task.

Step 4 – Create your calendar. Now it is time to pick the three marketing activities you are going to be implementing first. How you choose the activities is up to you, but personally, I like to start with the activities I feel are going to make me the most money the fastest so I have additional capital to fund the other ideas on my list. Once you have chosen your first three activities, assign each step to a person on staff or another company, or add the activity to your calendar. Once on your calendar, you need to treat it like any other appointment and make sure you keep the appointment you set with yourself and follow through on the task you scheduled. If the marketing activity is something that you will be doing over and over again throughout the year, make sure you also schedule the future events. Once your schedule shows a marketing activity should be completed and working, add all of your tasks for the next marketing activity to your list, as well as include a list of tasks you are planning to assign, and then simply rinse and repeat.

At the end of the day, no plan, no matter how well thought out, will ever amount to anything more than words on paper if you don't take action and implement. For those that you do implement, you may find some work great and others are duds, but at the end of the year, when you implement, your sales will have increased and your business will be more stable than it was 12 short months ago.

CHAPTER 13
Use of Celebrities in a Newsletter

"The Newsletter Pro" May 2012 – Business Lessons from John Rich, Country Music Superstar and Winner of Celebrity Apprentice

It's not every day you get the chance to hear a country superstar speak and perform, much less meet him in person, but that is exactly what happened to me at the end of April. In case you are not familiar with John Rich, he is half of the country act Big and Rich, the band behind popular songs such as "Save a Horse, Ride a Cowboy" and "The 8th of November." If you are one of the few Celebrity Apprentice fans left, you'll recognize him as last year's winner. Like many celebrities, John has an amazing rags-to-riches story, but unlike so many famous people, John is also a good businessman. Here are just a few business lessons I took away from my meeting with John Rich.

1. **Nothing beats celebrity.** The power of celebrity to open doors and command obscene prices for just about anything is second only to the federal government's. So, that begs the question, how can you leverage celebrity to help your business grow? I will write more on this topic in an upcoming issue.

2. **If it's worth having, it won't come easy.** John talked about how he wrote over 500 songs before he sold a single one. He attributed much of his success to the fact that he simply would not give up. Have you ever noticed that on TV all the world's problems seem to be solved in an hour? On the hit TV show 24, Jack Bauer was able to save the world in just under 24 hours, eight separate times! Real life simply doesn't move that fast, and because of that, most of us give up on our dreams far too early.

3. **Take care of your fans.** John spoke at length about how much he tries to interact personally with as many of his fans as possible. Sometimes it is simply via Twitter; sometimes he spends hours before or after a concert signing autographs. He recognizes his fame and success is due to the fans. Many business owners forget about their existing customers and focus solely on getting new customers. For most companies, this mistake

leaves bundles of money on the table because they're ignoring existing customers. It is important to tend to your existing clients before you try to add new ones.

4. **Give back.** On Celebrity Apprentice, John raised the most money in the history of the show for his charity. It was obvious when hearing him speak how important it is to him to give back. Too many people think of business owners as greedy, but many are not that way. In fact, some of the most successful business owners I know are also some of the biggest givers of both time and money.

I thoroughly enjoyed my time with John Rich and the lessons he shared. Not to mention, nothing beats having a proven superstar lay out a fairly simply road map for success that anyone can follow. Enjoy the rest of the newsletter, and I'll talk to you next month.

CHAPTER 14
Business-to-Consumer Sample Articles

Article from "The Monthly Smile" August 2012

Fun Summer Adventures

My wife and I recently decided to get out of our comfort zones and try something new. We competed in the first ever Ponderosa Pine Relay Race this past month. My wife has really gotten into running over the past year and has participated in three half marathons (Race to Robie Creek was her first), but this was the first relay race either one of us had ever done. We joined a team of 12 people and agreed to run three legs each (which ranged from three to 10 miles long). The race, which started in Weiser, went through McCall and eventually ended in Cascade.

Part of the challenge of these kinds of races is adapting

to the elements and the rural surroundings. The weather was brutally hot, and my wife relied greatly on the aid vans (which followed the runners through the race and handed them water and sports drinks) to keep her hydrated during her first leg. On my first leg, I wasn't so lucky. It was down a narrow dirt road that the aid vans were not able to navigate safely, so I was on my own, with only my water belt to keep me going. It was a nine-mile leg, and around mile six, I drained the last two ounce bottle on my belt. Let me tell you, a three-mile run in 90-plus degree heat with absolutely zero water is as much a mental challenge as it is a physical one. I was running along the river at this point and was so thirsty that I even considered popping down to the water's edge to get something to drink and cool off. I was worried I wouldn't be able to make the climb back up, so I decided against it. Eventually, I made it to the end of the leg. Tired and thirsty, I guzzled down as much water as I could once back in the van. My second leg was equally eventful. It was on an unmarked trail, and I literally found myself yelling out loud in a meager attempt to keep bears away throughout the entire thing. The upside was, the fear of being eaten by a wild animal took my mind off running. I guess in that type of situation, any distraction is a good distraction.

When all was said and done, our team crossed the finish line around 3:00 p.m. on Saturday (we started in Weiser at 8:00 a.m. on Friday). It's amazing the way adrenaline can push your body, no matter how tired you are. The feeling of knowing we had accomplished such a cool thing together was incredibly rewarding. The entire thing was a great bonding experience for my wife and I, and we got to know the other 10 members of our team very well over the course of the weekend. Some of the best times were just sitting in the van laughing, joking, and cheering on our team member that was running. We were sore for a few days following the race, but it was a small price to pay for such a great experience. We will definitely be competing in the Ponderosa Pine Relay again.

The girls were proud of us for our accomplishment, but opted to stay home. They are busy preparing to go back to school this month. It's hard to believe another summer has already come and gone! They are excited to get back into the swing of things with school and fall sports. And we as a family are excited for slightly cooler weather and watching some BYU football. I hope you all are enjoying the last days of August with your friends and family!

Article from "On Your Side" – Halloween: A Family Tradition

Every family has time-honored traditions that they look forward to each year. In my family, our favorite holiday is Halloween, without a doubt. All of our extended family lives in or around the Atlanta area, so Christmas and Thanksgiving are always spent traveling between the homes of our loved ones. Halloween is the one holiday where we actually don't go anywhere. For the past seven years, we have turned Halloween into a big event by turning our house into a haunted house. We do a maze in the garage, my wife takes care of all the amazing decorations and holiday-themed food, and we love to just have a good time with our family, friends, and neighbors. We open up the house to the public, and people actually travel from pretty far around to come check out our haunted party—it's pretty cool!

We set up the haunted house to be perfect for kids from about age 6 to 9 (scary, but not too scary!). And our own kids, Noah and Sam (ages 10 and 8), have come to look forward to Halloween the way many kids look forward to Santa Clause's visit (not that they aren't excited for him to come too, but we'll talk about that more next month). They both start wanting to decorate for the party as soon as October rolls around. We actually had to make it a rule that decorations are not allowed to go up before then. Otherwise, we would have cobwebs and skeletons around our house 365 days a year! This year, we had some great new additions to our collection of spooky décor—a blown-up pumpkin carriage and horse! They were a big hit at the party. Our family always gets into character for the party as well, and this year, we were a family of zombies! The menu this year included marshmallow mummies, spider cupcakes, tombstone brownies, and even black cats made out of Ho-Ho's.

Everyone had a blast, and we loved getting to share our favorite tradition with old friends, and new ones. This year, several people from the office brought their kids as well. We are always looking to expand our ideas for the haunted house, so if you happen to have any, we would love to hear them. And come next Halloween if you find yourself in the Peach Tree City area, make the trip over to our house and join in the fun.

Article from "Doggone Dental Digest" August 2012 – The Doggone Truth According to Nestle Part 2

Hi, it's Nestle again. Last month I shared our trip to the doggie doctor with you and a few other things about me. This month we are going to discuss my title of "Doggie ATM," the tale of Puppy Boot Camp, my take on duck hunting, and one of our latest Ebony stories.

Let's get started with my title of "Doggie ATM." When I was a puppy, I was a little mischievous, but nowhere near as much trouble as Moose and Ebony. Anyway, one of my favorite things to get ahold of was a thing that Mom and Dad call wallets. They tend to be made of a material called leather and are a little like rawhide chews. I would get ahold of usually Dad's wallet because Mom puts hers into a thing that she calls a purse and that is miserable to try to get into because it has a zipper. Dad, on the other hand, had a tendency to leave his wallet on the bathroom counter. That is an easy target. One day, I was able to sneak, which really is not has hard as you might think in our house, into the bathroom and grab Dad's wallet. Well, inside this thing, there are some papers that have a smell like Dad. Mom says that it is because Dad touches them. My favorite thing is not to tear apart the wallet but to get the papers in the wallet. Mom told me that it is paper, known as money, and that they use it to get us dog food. Now who would want to give up some really good dog food for some of this paper? I really don't understand it, but I am thankful that the exchange takes place because I love to eat! So the other thing to know about these papers is that they have numbers on them. My favorites are the ones that have a number that looks like 10 and 20, but the best one ever was the one that had a 50 on it. Dad was really upset to find one of those missing. He even spent time out in the dog pen looking through the dog poop for any sign of that bill. Well, he found it, but apparently there was an incomplete serial number so they could not exchange it for a new 50. Apparently, the place known as the bank, where this stuff called money comes from, will not give you a different bill unless there is one entire serial number on it. I don't know how many serial numbers a bill has, but it must be more than one. Oh boy, did I ever hear about that incident. Good thing is that Mom and Dad may get mad, but they do not tend to stay that way long. We really love that about them. They are great parents in that regard.

One thing that none of my siblings told you (probably because the younger dogs don't really know about it) is that I actually got kicked out of Puppy Boot Camp. You see, when I was little, Mom and Dad both worked full-time. Now Mom works from home part-time, so things are different. Anyway, for the first couple of months, we were sent down to Grandpa Paul's house (aka Puppy Boot Camp) so we could be house trained. Well, I was referred to as the "land shark" because I would bite everything. I loved my toys and anything else I could sink my teeth into. I remember being told "No bites." I seem to sense a theme in my life, No, No, No, No. You get the idea. Anyway, after about a month, Grandpa Paul had to call Dad to tell him he just had to take me home because I was too much of a terror to live with Grandpa Paul. So he came down and got me. After failing at Puppy Boot Camp and going home for a few months, I was sent to a place to learn how to hunt.

Being at hunter school was kind of neat. I was able to see the state known as Texas for one winter. I really liked that because it was the year of no winter. Literally, it never got cold that year, and I never saw any of the stuff they call snow. You know, the white stuff that falls from above. (The replacement for the wet stuff that falls from above the rest of the year, Mom says that it is called rain.) Anyway, learning to hunt is hard. Lucky was the best at it (although he is not a very good swimmer.) Personally, I just want to go get the birds when I see them. Why the heck wait until they tell you to "get the bird"? The way I see it, if the bird is out there, why can't I just go get it for them before they make those things called guns make the loud sound? Seems to me we could just cut out the noise and get on with things. When I was with the trainer, I did a better job of listening and only going to get the bird on command. When there are 4 or 5 of us out hunting, it is really fun because they cannot shoot the guns and hold on to us until they want us to go, and Mom cannot hold on to all of us at one time. We have a blast, especially Hershey and me. Hershey is a much better swimmer than me, and Dad says that she has a more gentle mouth. I just don't want that darn bird to get away from me once I catch up to it!

The birds that are the most difficult to hunt are referred to as "divers." Believe me when I tell you that is exactly what they do. They dive under the water, and you have to swim around in circles until they resurface. Dad, Grandpa, Uncle Greg, Brian, and the boys are pretty good at watching with us and then telling us with hand and verbal commands where the bird surfaced so we can get back on our mission. We have not been hunting for a few years. I think that Mom gets pretty tired of trying to control us, and the last couple of times we were hunting we did not see many birds. So, anyway, I think you get the idea of hunting. It is a lot of hard work, and our tails don't work for a day or so after we have been out hunting. But boy, oh boy, is it a blast! I am sure Hershey will tell you a little more about hunting as well.

Finally, one of our Ebony tales. I cannot remember what Dad was doing, but one day he took this blue box out of the cleaning closet and put it on the lower kitchen counter. See, in our house, they have a center island that has the thing called the sink and a contraption called a dishwasher that makes a lot of noise (they think it is quiet, but they don't hear like we do). The center island also has an upper level. I think I have heard Mom call it a breakfast bar. Dad put the blue box on the lower counter. Then he took two blue things out of the box and proceeded to put them on his hands. Mom said they are rubber gloves. Apparently, Dad uses them all the time at his job. We have boxes and boxes and boxes of these blue things at our house, and from time to time, Dad will take them to his work. Anyway, Dad walked away from the blue box, and Ebony got mad because he left her with us instead of letting her go with him to do whatever it was he had to do. Well, she put her front feet on the lower counter and grabbed the blue box. She took it to the bedroom. She jumped up on to the bed with the box and proceeded to destroy and somewhat eat the box. She said that the glove things did not taste very good, but she had a good time tearing some of them up. Anyway, she had box pieces all over the bed, and needless to say, when the box was no longer around the blue gloves, the gloves went everywhere. Dad was not very happy when he found Ebony and her treasures.

Next month, you will hear from Hershey. I am sure that she will tell you a story about her experience hunting, and I am sure that Ebony or Moose will get into something between now and then.

Until we talk next, take care!

CHAPTER 15
My Challenge To You

The death of any good idea is time. Too often I meet people who told me six or twelve months ago that they wanted to get a newsletter started but for one reason or another they haven't done it. Like, you know, they understand the benefits but don't take action, and at the end of the day, nothing happens until someone takes action.

My challenge to you is to take action. You know how powerful newsletters are and how they can change your business if you use them.

A good first start would be to go to my website and get a free premium subscription to our newsletter, plus a free copy of our Gold CD. I have put the details of the offer on the next page...

Special Bonus!
If you haven't already done so, start right now by going to my website to receive a FREE 12-month premium print subscription to my monthly newsletter, plus a bonus copy of one of my Gold CDs titled "5 Ways to Use Newsletters to Increase Sales and Crush Your Competition." Both complement this book well. Just go to www.TheNewsletterpro.com/book and fill in the form on the screen. We'll mail (yes, a real physical hard copy of both the newsletter and CD will be mailed to you). Go to www.TheNewsletterpro.com/book. You'll be happy you did!

Made in the USA
Charleston, SC
03 August 2013